Electronics and control systems

JAMES SAGE • DAVID S.C. THOMPSON

SERIES EDITORS: PETER BRANSON • JONATHAN RENAUDON-SMITH

CAMBRIDGE
UNIVERSITY PRESS

Published by the Press Syndicate of the University of Cambridge
The Pitt Building, Trumpington Street, Cambridge CB2 1RP
40 West 20th Street, New York, NY 10011-4211, USA
10 Stamford Road, Oakleigh, Melbourne 3166, Australia

© Cambridge University Press 1996

First published 1996

Produced by Gecko Limited, Granville Way, Bicester, Oxon

Printed in Great Britain at the University Press, Cambridge

A catalogue record for this book is available from the British Library

ISBN 0 521 49961 5

Cover – Robotic arm.

Cover design by Ralf Zeigermann

Acknowledgements

The authors and publisher would like to thank the following
for their assistance during the writing of this book.

Association for Science Education/Design and Technology
Association *Science with Technology* units: *Understanding
sensors, Understanding control, Investigating and designing
control systems*;
Sean Crawford;
Michael Duffy;
Electricity Supply Board;
Eurotunnel;
Glaxo Wellcome plc;
J Sainsbury plc;
Hewlett Packard;
John Rooney;
Royal National Institute for the Blind;
Staff at Cathaleen's Fall and Cliff Power Stations and ESB
Headquarters, Dublin;
Robert Worsley.

The publisher would like to thank the following for
permission to reproduce copyright photographs.

Art Directors Photo Library 69;
Donald Cooper Photostage 75;
Donald Smith 70;
Dr Michael Wyndham 50, 51, 61;
Graham Portlock 7, 11, 14–15, 30, 76, 78, 79, 88;
J. Madere/ZEFA Cover;
Jeremy Hoare/Life File 65;
Michael Rosenfeld/Tony Stone Images 73;
QA Photos 74;
Robert Harding Picture Library 68.

Contents

The product development process

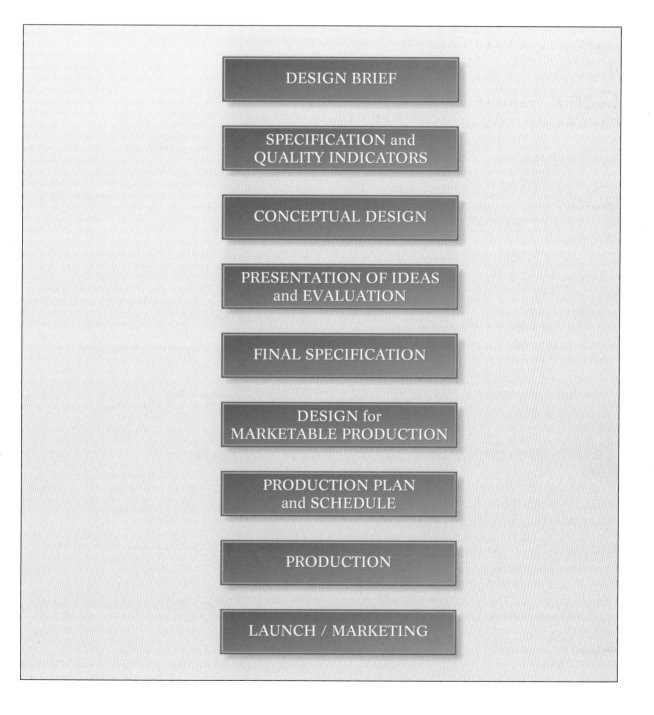

Systems

The word **system** is commonly used – for example, we talk about traffic systems, weather systems and hi-fi systems. This book will consider both electronic and computer control systems. We use special terms to describe systems, so we shall talk about these terms in this chapter.

A thorough way to define a system is to use the following four-point description. All four points have to apply if something can be considered to be a system:

- the system is made up of parts or activities that do something,
- the parts or activities are connected together in an organised way,
- the parts or activities affect what is going through the system, so that it is changed when it leaves the system,
- the whole thing has been identified by humans as of interest.

(The Open University)

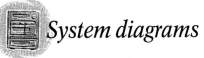 ## System diagrams

A useful way of looking at systems is to put an imaginary box or **boundary** around the system. The boundary defines the limits of the system. Where the system boundary is placed depends on what aspect of the system you want to look at – inside the boundary is the system you want to look at, outside is the environment in which the system works. The boundary box will contain the **processes** that the system undertakes. There will also be **inputs** to and **outputs** from the system – these will cross over the boundary.

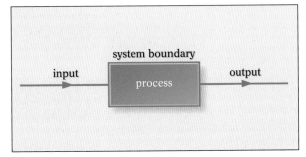

▲ *A system.*

When you first consider a system, there is no need to provide a detailed explanation of how the processes within the system actually work. The processes are described by the relationship between the inputs and the outputs, that is the *function* of the system. For example, in a food processor, food chunks are inputs and liquidised food is the output!

Describe the following in terms of input, output and function:
- a television,
- a vacuum cleaner,
- a hairdrier,
- a computer.

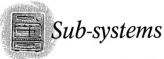 ## Sub-systems

A **sub-system** is a functional part of a larger system. A complex system can be modelled by splitting the larger system into sub-systems. Although the process inside the boundary may be complex, you can still represent it by a straightforward sequence of actions. This makes the processes inside the system easier to understand. You can then think of each sub-system as being made up of lower sub-systems, each of which can be described as a system in its own right. The lower the level of the sub-system, the more likely it is that you will be able to understand its function. For example, a low-level sub-system within a JCB excavator would be a simple lever mechanism.

Before you start to draw input–process–output system diagrams, you should decide what type of system you are looking at. Is it, for example, an information processing system, a metal processing system, an energy processing system or a food processing system?

> Give examples of these types of system. List some other types of system.

Remember, the sub-systems approach is intended to make it easier for you to understand a complex system.

A drinks machine

▲ *A machine for dispensing drinks.*

▼ *A system and its sub-systems. System A has B, C and D as its sub-systems and system D has E and F as its sub-systems.*

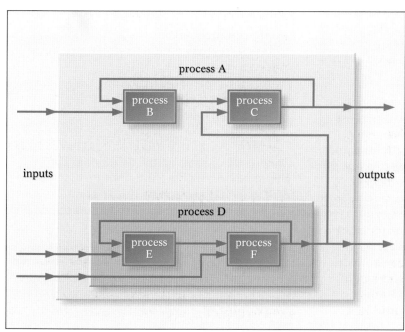

Soft-drinks machines are now very common. They often have a selection of up to ten different cans of drink to choose from. It is possible to draw a model or *flow-block diagram* of the drinks machine. Such a model is shown on page 8. The arrows represent signals, or something moving or flowing.

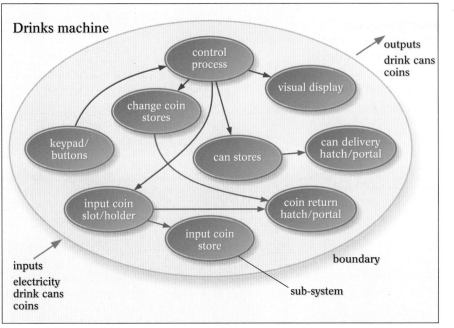

A model of a soft-drinks machine.

The machine is shown as having a boundary, inputs (influences from the surroundings that affect the machine) and outputs (influences that the machine has on its surroundings). Some of the sub-systems within the machine are shown inside the boundary. The lines drawn between these sub-systems show that one sub-system influences another.

> What influences have been left out?
> Why do you think they have been left out?

A systems approach is used to model a machine or process in order to make the whole process easier to understand. It should reduce a complex machine or process to a simpler model or models. Any model does not need to show all the details, but it should contain all the parts that are relevant to you.

Our model of the drinks machine is only one way in which the machine may be described. For example, the can stores could be shown as separate parts and the control process could be shown as separate mechanical, electronic, electrical, and pneumatic control processes.

> What do the blue arrows show in the diagram?
> What do the red arrows show?
> What is it that the control process does?

Sequences

With a soft-drinks machine the customer works through a series of actions to get a drink:

1 put in enough money,
2 press the cancel button to stop the actions if necessary,
3 press the correct drink button,
4 take the drink delivered,
5 take any change.

A series of events like this is often referred to as a **sequence** or programme of actions. The simple sequence above does not include actions to be taken if the machine does not return your coins, delivers the wrong can or does not deliver the change.

> Make a list of the actions that you think will take place inside the machine when you have put in some coins. You might be allowed to have a look inside one of the machines in your school.

Flow charts

Each block in your system diagram should contain very little detail and may represent a set of complex sub-systems. Flow-block diagrams are very useful for showing how the parts of a system link up. Some of these sub-systems may be further explored using **flow charts**.

A flow chart may be used to illustrate a sequence of actions such as those of the customer using the drinks machine. Flow charts can be used to describe parts of a system in greater detail.

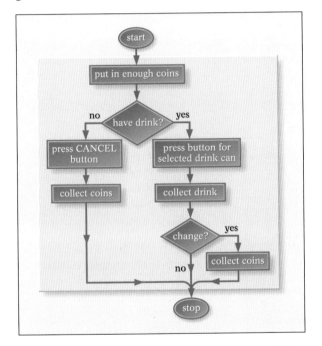

▲ *A flow chart of the actions of a customer which could represent part of the can and change delivery sub-system in the drinks machine.*

A sequence of actions described by a flow chart is called a **procedure**.

More about ... procedures page 39.

The flow chart on the right shows the control system for the drinks machine. A cancel procedure, that also clears the display on the drinks machine, is placed between connectors A and B. The connections shown between C

and D link to a delivery procedure that delivers the drink and calculates and delivers the correct change.

Copy and complete the flow chart for the sections between: A and B, C and D. What do you think goes between E and F?

▼ *Flow chart for the drinks machine control system.*

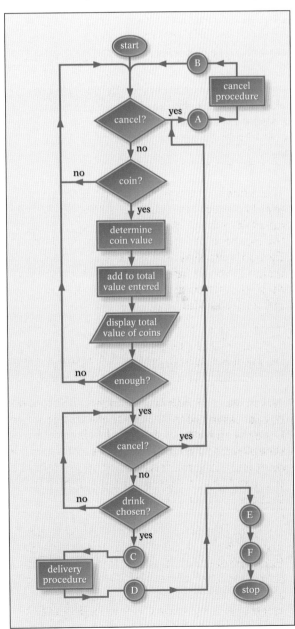

Suppose that there are two newsagents near your house. Draw a simple flow chart to show how you would fetch an evening paper. Your flow chart could allow for various options and choices:
- how far it is to the nearest newsagent,
- what to do if one is closed,
- what to do if both newsagents were closed when you reached them.

Sensors and transducers

Sensors and **transducers** are devices that are affected by their surroundings. Sensors and transducers are used to provide a way by which information may enter or leave the control system.

Transducer	Type	Energy conversion
thermocouple	input	heat to electrical energy
photocell	input	light to electrical energy
dynamo or generator	input	movement (kinetic energy) to electrical energy
microphone	input	sound to electrical energy
heating coil	output	electrical energy to heat
lamp	output	electrical energy to light
motor	output	electrical energy to movement (kinetic energy)
loudspeaker	output	electrical energy to sound

Some sensors used in electronics are affected by their surroundings so that their electrical properties change; for example, their resistance may increase. Examples of these sensors are:

- light-dependent resistors (their resistance depends on the amount of light falling on them),
- thermistors (their resistance depends on temperature),
- potentiometers (their resistance depends on the the position of a control – for example, the volume control on an amplifier),
- tuning capacitors (their capacities depend on the position of a control).

Transducers convert energy from one form to another. In electronic systems, you will often use transducers as output devices, although there are also input transducers.

The flow chart for the drinks machine on page 9 includes actions such as 'determine coin value' and 'display total value of coins'. These actions can be carried out by electronic systems using sensors and transducers.

More about ... electronic sensors and output devices pages 92–101.

To understand how an electronic system might be useful in a drinks machine, think about the electronic system that displays the value of an inserted coin. The display must stay blank if no coin has been inserted. The display must show the correct value of coins when they are inserted. Draw a flow chart that describes these actions.

The diagram on page 11 shows one way in which electronics can be used to detect coins and display the value of the coins detected. See how some parts of this diagram have been drawn across the electronic system boundary.

Which parts of this system could be wholly electronic?
Which parts of the system are not wholly electronic? Why have some parts been drawn across the boundary?

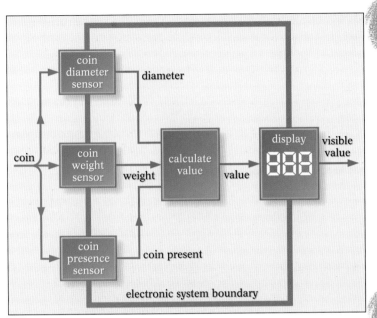

▲ *Coin value display system.*

Suggest possible designs for sensing:
- the diameter of the coin,
- the weight of the coin,
- the presence of the coin.

How many sensors do you think you need?
What is the least number of sensors you need?
Design a sensor to do all of the above functions.

◀ *A McDonald's restaurant.*

Interfacing

The form of a signal at the output of one sub-system must match exactly the form of signal required at the input of another sub-system. For example, coins dropped into a slot in a drinks machine cannot by themselves make the display show the correct value. The coin detector or sensor must produce a signal that the display can 'understand' and use. This process of matching signals between sub-systems is often referred to as **signal conditioning** or *interfacing*.

A fast-food restaurant

In this section you will meet further ideas to do with systems. These are **feedback, open-** and **closed-loop control** and **lag**. Looking at how a fast-food restaurant operates is a good way of showing what these ideas mean. You will need to understand these ideas, and use them when you come to design and make your electronic and control systems.

A fast-food restaurant can be considered as a complex system.

Draw a flow-block diagram showing how the activities affect each other in a fast-food restaurant. It may help to work in a group for this activity.

It may be easier to understand what a fast-food restaurant does by listing its inputs and outputs. The table shows an example of such a list.

Inputs	Outputs
start-up/development capital loan	repayments on start-up loan, including interest
food materials	prepared food
packaging and containers	waste
customers	satisfied customers
energy – electricity, oil, gas	heat, light, sound
water	drainage/sewerage
cleaning materials	salaries
advertising and marketing consultants	publicity and display materials
food technology consultants	consultancy fees
managerial staff	managerial staff
non-managerial staff	non-managerial staff
income from sales	bank account credits, including profits
customer comments	taxes
new equipment	faulty or obsolete equipment
maintenance and repair of equipment	bill payments

What is the main purpose of a fast-food restaurant?

What are the main activities that enable the purpose to be fulfilled?

Name some of the process systems that enable the restaurant to operate. These process systems use the inputs and produce the outputs. For example, money coming in from sales requires an accounting system before it is sent to the bank to be credited to the restaurant.

Make a list of the criteria that you could use to judge if the restaurant has been successful at meeting its purpose. These criteria should be simple statements against which the success of the restaurant can be judged. For example, standards of cleanliness, efficiency of service and value for money.

Open-loop control
If the restaurant were operated without taking any account of performance, it would be said to use an open-loop control system. The control process would carry on even in the absence of customers' comments or profits, until external influences such as the bank or the shareholders intervened. A system operating open-loop control has no **feedback**.

More about ... open-loop control pages 26–29.

What open-loop systems are used in a fast-food restaurant?

Can you think of any other open-loop systems?

Closed-loop control
Feedback is the name given to information produced by the system that is used to change the way a system operates. Information from the output of a system may be used to modify the input to the system. In the fast-food restaurant, comments from the customers and financial information from the money processing system will provide an indication of how the restaurant is performing. Performance outputs such as customer satisfaction and profit can be used to modify the operation of the restaurant and may cause increased profit, further customer satisfaction, a reduction in waste, and so on. For example, if the number of customers using the

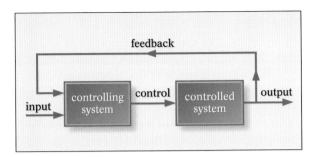

▲ *Feedback in a closed-loop system.*

restaurant falls, changing the menu or the decor might lead to an increase in customers, replacing the table sugar with counter sachets might reduce waste and save staff time.

A system operating closed-loop control can have either *positive feedback* or *negative feedback*.

Positive feedback

Positive feedback responds to an increase in the output by changing the input in such a way that the output is further increased. For example, suppose a fast-food restaurant produces a very good product. Sales should increase and this would indicate that even more of the product should be made. The control system would recognise that sales were higher than predicted and would decide that more products should be made. This could go on for ever. However, this situation is unlikely to become unstable because other effects could come into play.

> What other controlling effects could be called into play?

In electronic and other control systems, positive feedback usually results in a system becoming unstable, so it is often avoided.

Negative feedback

Negative feedback works to change the input in such a way that the output is decreased to a stable level.

In the fast-food restaurant, one of the controlling effects is customer choice. For

example, after a while the customers will want to try other food products, and sales of a once-popular product will decrease. The control system would recognise that sales were lower than predicted and would decide that fewer products should be made. Eventually only enough products will be made to satisfy the demand. The production will reach a stable state.

Negative feedback is often used in electronic and control systems to maintain stable operation of these systems.

A food quality control system

Information gathered from the customers to measure the performance of the restaurant is known as customer feedback. The company may use *market research* techniques to obtain this information. This will help them to maintain or improve the quality of their products and service.

Customer feedback may show:

- how many people use the restaurant and at what time,
- how much money the restaurant takes each day, week or month,
- how much of each type of food is sold each day, week or month.

This will help the company plan how many staff they need, how much food they need to order, how much they pay for the food materials they use, and so on.

> Can you think of any other feedback that would be useful to maintain the quality of the food produced?

Error signal

In a system with feedback, the difference between the input signal and the feedback signal is called the **error signal**. The size of the error signal determines how much the system output is changed. When the system is near a stable state, the error signal will be almost zero. This is because very little change needs to be made to keep the system stable. When the system is a long way from being stable, the error signal will be large and this will cause a large change in the control signal.

In the fast-food restaurant, an example of an error signal is the difference between the projected sales figures and the actual sales figures. If sales are higher than projected, the error signal is positive causing the production to increase. If sales are lower than projected, the error signal is negative causing the production to decrease.

Hunting

Hunting is where a system with feedback constantly misses reaching a stable state. The final state is first too far away from stability in one direction, and then too far away in the other direction. For example, the food quality in the restaurant is too high one week, too low the next, too high the next, and so on. Another example is balancing on a beam: first you correct your balance one way, only to find a moment later you have to correct your balance the other way to stop you falling.

Suggest other systems where hunting may occur.

Lag

It takes time for a system to respond to feedback signals. For example, if customer feedback suggests a need for a new food item on the menu, it will take time to develop the new item and provide it to the restaurant. This time delay is known as **lag**. It is caused because the system is unable to respond immediately. Lag exists to some degree in all closed-loop systems. For example, there is a lag between:

- designers identifying and generating new ideas and the product being available to consumers,
- you feeling hungry and being able to satisfy that hunger,
- you turning up the heating control at home and the house reaching the required temperature (see pages 26–28 for activity about this).

Think about some of the other processes in the fast-food restaurant. For each process, explain why lag might occur and the effect it will have on the system. Suggest other examples of lag in real life.

You should now know about:
- **representing systems using flow-block diagrams and flow charts,**
- **analysing systems as processes with inputs and outputs,**
- **breaking down a complex system into a series of linked sub-systems,**
- **the terms used when describing systems,**
- **how the output can be used to control the input using feedback.**

You should now be able to complete the task below, which may form part or all of your coursework.

Choose one of the systems mentioned below.
- A telephone network.
- A computer.
- A modern hospital.
- A car engine.
- A food production factory.

1 Identify the influences on the system.
2 Describe the system in terms of input–process–output.
3 Draw a flow-block diagram to represent the system.
4 Draw a boundary around one aspect of the system that you want to investigate further and use flow charts to represent what is going on.

The Erne Hydroelectric Development

Natural water systems (rivers, lakes, etc.) are often used as energy storage systems. Stored water is used to turn turbines to create electricity in a hydroelectric power station. A dam is often built to retain a large volume of water in a reservoir. The water flow out of the reservoir is directed and controlled to the point where the hydroelectric power station is built.

This chapter looks at a hydroelectric development of the Electricity Supply Board (ESB) on the River Erne in the Republic of Ireland. It shows how systems thinking and systems design are used in a real situation.

▼ *Map of the area around the Erne Hydroelectric Development.*

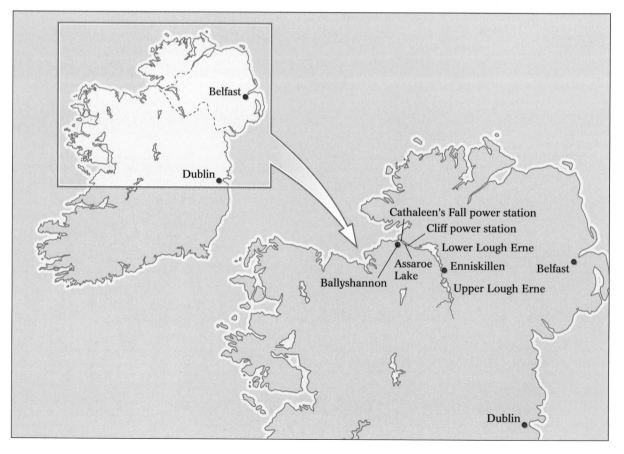

The Erne Hydroelectric Development (consisting of two hydroelectric power stations) is in Ballyshannon in the Republic of Ireland. It was opened in 1952. This development has two dams: one at Cliff, beside a town called Belleek, and another at Cathaleen's Fall in Ballyshannon, a few miles or so before the River Erne enters the Atlantic Ocean. The two power stations were built on the stretch of river between Belleek and the sea at Ballyshannon, making use of a natural drop in height of 45 m.

Building the two dams involved major construction and excavation work. Each power station has a *headrace* to direct the flow of water. A 1379 m long *tailrace*, or water outflow channel, was excavated from rock below Cathaleen's Fall Dam. The total water storage of the River Erne and its lakes is approximately 194 million cubic metres. The average flow of the river is 92 cubic metres per second (92 m^3/s) which can rise to over 400 cubic metres per second in a major flood. The *head of water* (the vertical difference between the levels of water above and below a power station) at Cliff is 10 m, and at Cathaleen's Fall it is 28.5 m.

To improve water control in the area, the 6 km long Belleek Channel was enlarged by excavating 600 000 cubic metres of earth and rock from the river bed, and a barrage and boat locks were constructed at Enniskillen. The Belleek Channel acts as a *flow limiter* between Lower Lough Erne and Cathaleen's Fall.

An influence diagram shows the main areas of interest in the Erne Hydroelectric Development, and illustrates how the parts of the development influence each other.

Originally the Erne Hydroelectric Development was controlled by a staff of 70 from control rooms at the Cathaleen's Fall and Cliff sites. The system was totally manual, with individual panel-mounted gauges and control switches and knobs – usually one panel per sub-system. Over the years, electronic and computer control systems have done away with much of the manual work. The computer control systems now monitor and control:

- the turbines,
- the generators,
- spillway gates,
- fishpass gates,
- smolt gates,
- cooling water systems,
- the headrace and tailrace at both plants.

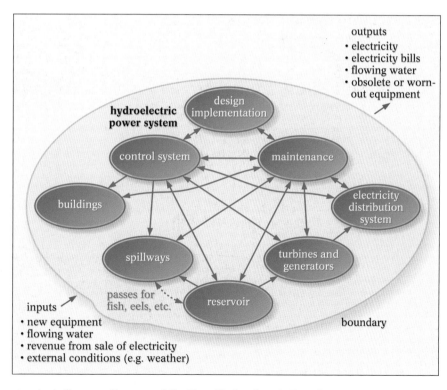

▲ *An influence diagram of the Erne Hydroelectric Development.*

What is the purpose of the Erne Hydroelectric Development system?

What are the inputs to this system?

What are the outputs of the Erne Hydroelectric Development?

What type of sensors do you think might be needed for the conditions being monitored and controlled?

More about ... sensors pages 92–97.

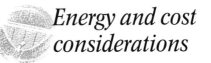

Plant description

The upper station at Cliff and the lower power station at Cathaleen's Fall each have two turbines driving electrical generators.

Screens are placed in front of the water intake at the headrace to stop debris entering the *penstock*. (The penstock is the channel taking water from the headrace to the turbines.) These screens have to be cleaned regularly because they become blocked with debris, which reduces the flow of water into the penstock.

Energy and cost considerations

Since the stations opened in 1952, the money invested to construct the Erne Hydroelectric Development has been recovered from operating profits. The running costs are now salaries, repairs and maintenance, and overall improvement and development – there is no

▼ *Cross-section of Cathaleen's Fall generating station.*

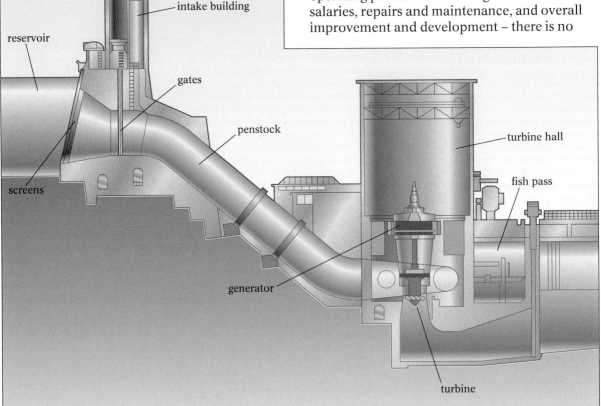

reservoir

intake building

gates

penstock

screens

turbine hall

fish pass

generator

turbine

outstanding loan to be paid off. As a result, the Erne Hydroelectric Development is generating electricity at approximately 0.5 pence per unit, which is much cheaper than electricity generated by any other means in Ireland.

The following table shows a comparison of approximate costs for generating electricity by different means.

Type of power station	Generating cost/pence per unit of electricity
fuel oil	1.4
natural gas	2.2
coal	3.2
hydroelectric	0.5
wind	5.0

In June 1995, an electricity grid link was re-established between the Republic of Ireland and Northern Ireland, from Ballyshannon to Enniskillen. This is one of a number of grid links between the two states. These links allow the ESB and Northern Ireland Electricity (NIE) to sell surplus electricity to each other. This enables them to reduce the number of stand-by generators (used at times of high demand) in Ireland as a whole.

Research the following.
- What is a unit of electricity?
- How does the cost of producing electricity at the Erne Hydroelectric Development compare with the cost of electricity supplied to your house (look at the latest electricity bill)?
- Energy from the River Erne is being used to generate electricity. Do you think this affects the river?
- How is this use of energy significant to this area environmentally, economically, and socially?

The local environment

The area is almost completely rural with an economy based on farming, fishing and tourism. Leisure activities, in particular boating and fishing, are now encouraged on Assaroe Lake, the reservoir for Cathaleen's Fall station, which was formed as part of the Erne Hydroelectric Development.

The River Erne was always good for salmon and eels. This meant that fishing became an important part of the local economy. Salmon migrate up rivers to produce their young, and the smolts (young salmon) then move down the rivers to the sea. Eels migrate down rivers, and produce their young in the Sargasso Sea (an area of the Atlantic Ocean); the elvers (young eels) return to the rivers to live. When dams are built on these rivers, the fish cannot move up or down the rivers, so no new generations of salmon or eels are produced. This is obviously bad for the fish, and is, in turn, damaging to the fish industry.

There has been a significant decline in salmon numbers in the Erne (partly due to the building and operation of the power stations), but this decline has been halted by the provision of a salmon hatchery at Cathaleen's Fall. This produces half a million smolts a year. A terraced set of tanks, 6 m long, 3 m wide and 1.25 m deep, (called a *salmon run*) are used to allow salmon and smolt to move past the dam. There are 73 tanks at Cathaleen's Fall. Each tank is connected to the next by an inclined pipe (about 0.5 m long and 0.7 m in diameter), through which water flows at the rate of 1 m^3/s. Salmon runs are monitored both by an automatic fish counter in Cathaleen's Fall fish pass and by inspection.

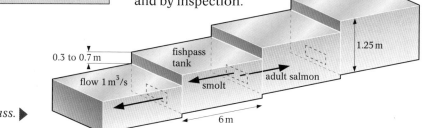

The fish pass. ▶

A chain of eel passes is also included at Cathaleen's Fall. This is different from the salmon run; eel passes are stony gullies with a steady, slow flow of water passing over the stones. The stones allow the small elvers (which are 2 to 8 cm long) to grip, and they climb to Assaroe Lake without becoming dry. It was found that once the elvers reach the new Assaroe Lake they did not need to travel further up the River Erne. To maintain the population balance within the River Erne and to improve stocks for fishing, the ESB (with co-operation from the Department of Agriculture for Northern Ireland) trap the elvers at Cathaleen's Fall. These elvers are then distributed throughout the river network. In 1995, 7.5 million elvers were trapped and distributed. The fish and eel passes are also protected from predators – people, mink, rats, birds and so on.

The fish counting system

Three pairs of electrodes, which are connected to a counter, are mounted in the connecting tubes between the tanks. When a fish moves between an electrode pair, the resistance between the electrodes drops. A salmon will pass through the tube in about 0.1 s. If a change in resistance is detected between electrode positions A and B, and then between B and C in this time, a fish is assumed to have moved upstream. The sensitivity of the unit can be adjusted; it is usually set to detect salmon with a

mass of approximately 2 kg. A glass panel in the side of the fish pass tank allows a person to confirm the reading on the electronic counter and to examine the state of the fish. An alternative video fish-detection and tape-recording system is being tested.

> What type of sensors could you use to detect movement?
> Could any of these be used in water?
> What modifications could you make to your sensor designs to make them suitable for use in water?

> **More about …** sensors pages 92–97.

> The adult salmon swim one way through the fish pass. Use a systems kit to design an electronic system that will only count objects moving one way.

Automatic control of the fish pass system

There are four fish pass gates and one smolt gate at Cathaleen's Fall. The salmon swim through one of these gates into Assaroe Lake. The fish pass gates are positioned at different heights in the dam wall. There can be only one gate open at a time, and this is chosen on the basis of the level of the water in the headrace. The lower the headrace, the lower the gate that is opened. These gates are either open or closed, and so require a **digital** closed-loop control system. This automatic control only takes place if the smolt gate is closed.

> **More about …** closed-loop control pages 12–13 and 108.

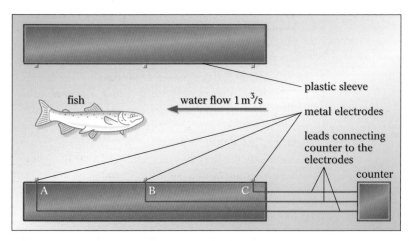

fish

water flow 1 m³/s

plastic sleeve

metal electrodes

leads connecting counter to the electrodes

counter

A   B   C

▲ *The fish sensing system.*

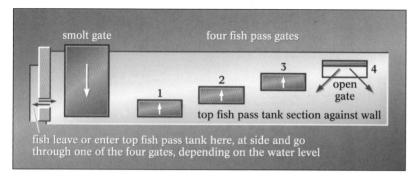

▲ *Fish pass and smolt gates at Cathaleen's Fall.*

Why are there four fish pass gates?
Why are the fish pass gate switching levels for rising water levels different from the switching levels for falling water levels?
Why is this a closed-loop control system?
Why must the smolt gate be closed before the fish pass gates work automatically?

Use an electronic systems kit to design and model a system that will open and close a sliding door automatically. You must make sure that when the door reaches the end of its travel it stops automatically. If the door is closed then pressing a button opens the door. If the door is open then pressing another button closes it. Can you arrange one button to do both functions?
The system you develop will mimic the action of one of the fish pass gates.
You may wish to develop this system, perhaps using computer control software to improve the flexibility of the system.

More about ... computer control pages 30–43.

▼ *Switching level for the fish pass gates at Cathaleen's Fall.*

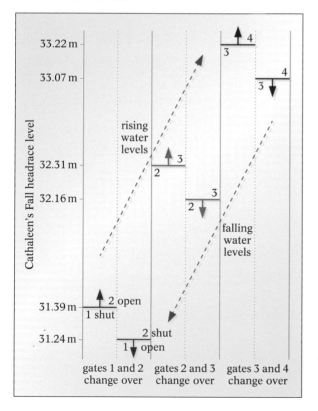

The water flow over the smolt gate is open to the air. Smolt are attracted to the flow of water over the smolt gate and enter the fish pass. Smolt travel with the flow from Assaroe Lake into the fish pass and on to the sea. The smolt gate is lowered to allow water to flow into the fish pass and is used to control the fish pass water level. This is achieved using closed-loop control. Because the height of the smolt gate can be set at any value between fully open and fully closed, the control system is **analogue**. The level of water in the fish pass is measured and fed back by electronics to the gate controller, which controls how far the smolt gate is opened. The gates cannot be lowered more than 0.6 m below the headrace level. This automatic control only takes place if all of the fish pass gates are closed.

Why must the fish pass gates be closed before the smolt gate works automatically?
Why is this a closed-loop control system?

Use an electronic systems kit to design a system that will open and close a swinging door. You must ensure that the door can take any position between fully closed and fully open. How far the door opens or closes is determined by the setting on a reference potentiometer.
The system you develop will mimic the action of the smolt gate.
You may wish to develop this system using computer control software.

More about ... potentiometers page 95.

More about ... computer control pages 30–43.

Name some digital control systems and some analogue control systems that you encounter in daily life.
For each control system, explain why you think an analogue or digital system was chosen.

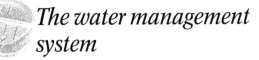

The water management system

Water management in the Erne Hydroelectric Development consists of making best use of the energy available in the stored water. It is important not to waste water, and maximum use must be made of the water in the Erne system. It is also important to keep the water levels in the system within certain limits.

What do the arrowed lines between the objects in this model of the Erne water system represent?
Is this a closed system (i.e. is there anything outside the boundary line which influences the system)?
If not, what are the inputs and/or outputs associated with the system?
What causes the loss of water from rivers, lakes, etc. to the atmosphere?
What affects the rate at which water may be lost?
What might be used to control the loss of water?

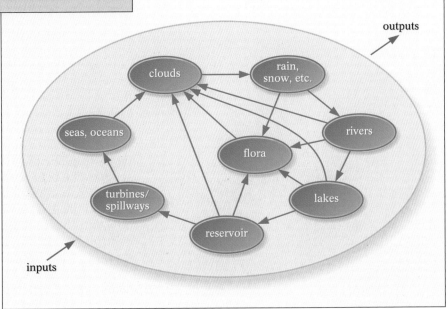

A model of the Erne ▶
water system.

Water-level monitoring

Water is drawn from the reservoir to generate electricity at Ballyshannon. As the rate of electricity generation is increased, so the rate at which the water is taken from the reservoir is increased. However, the dam has caused the overall levels in the water network to rise, particularly near the dam. The local community depends on the control system that ensures the water level is kept within manageable limits throughout the year.

The water level is monitored at three recorder stations in Northern Ireland, one on Upper Lough Erne at Bellisle, one at Enniskillen and one on Lower Lough Erne at Rosscor. Water levels at these stations may be obtained remotely at any time, because the signals from the water-level sensors can be accessed using the public telephone network.

▼ *Water level management – inputs to and outputs from the control system.*

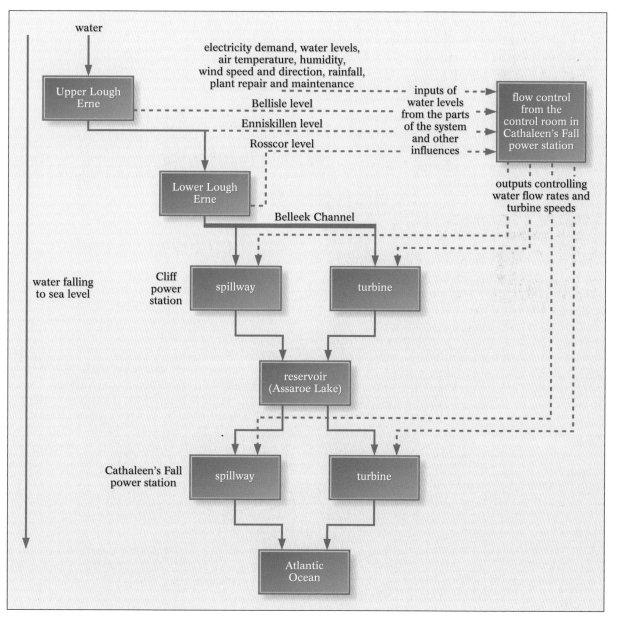

The diagram on page 23 shows the layout of the Erne system. The water-level monitoring points are shown both at the two power stations and upstream at the two Loughs.

> How would the system respond to:
> - prolonged periods of extremely heavy rainfall,
> - prolonged periods of extremely light rainfall,
> - the different seasons,
> - periods of exceptionally high demand?

There is no reason why the water levels at three monitoring points should be the same. For example, it is possible that, due to heavy rainfall, water levels in Upper Lough Erne could be rising while, due to the generation of electricity, levels in Lower Lough Erne are falling. There is a delay or **lag** in the system before water that falls in the hills is delivered to the reservoir. There is also a lag in the system before the withdrawal of water from the reservoir affects the water levels in the Loughs.

> **More about ...** lag page 14.

When there is heavy rainfall, the dam spillways may need to be opened to allow surplus water to be released from the reservoir. Otherwise upstream fields and roads could become flooded, crops and buildings could be damaged or destroyed, and animals might drown. If heavy rainfall is forecast sufficiently far in advance, water can be taken out of the reservoir by increasing water flow through the turbines. In this way, lag is allowed for and the extra water is not wasted – it is used to generate more electricity.

When there is low rainfall, the water run-off from the dam must be limited. This ensures that the water level in the system does not drop too far, which would cause the upstream water table to fall. This would result in river and canal banks falling in, and crops and animals suffering from lack of water. Also the structures of roads and buildings could suffer subsidence. Water in parts of the system must therefore be kept above certain levels.

> Use an electronic systems kit to design a system that monitors the level of water in a tank. The output could give a continuous signal that varies with the depth of water. Develop the system to produce a warning if the water level exceeds a maximum and/or a minimum level.

> Use an electronic systems kit to design a system that measures the flow of water through a channel or pipe. Develop the system to produce a warning if the water flow rate exceeds a maximum and/or a minimum flow rate. You may wish to develop this system using computer control software to improve the flexibility of the system.

> **More about ...** computer control pages 30–43.

The systems in the above activities mimic the action of the control systems in the Erne water level management system.

The automated control system

It will soon be possible to place the control consoles many miles from Cathaleen's Fall or Cliff, perhaps in Dublin. The stations at Cathaleen's Fall and Cliff would then need only a small (engineering) caretaker staff. This was not possible with the older manual system. As part of the remote operation, the development could be monitored by several closed circuit television (CCTV) cameras. The direction of view, the degree of zoom, lighting, and so on associated with these cameras would be operated from the control room.

> Use a computer to develop a program that will move a CCTV camera in the Erne system. The program must get the camera to scan an area continuously, starting at one point, returning to the same point and waiting a while before repeating the scan.

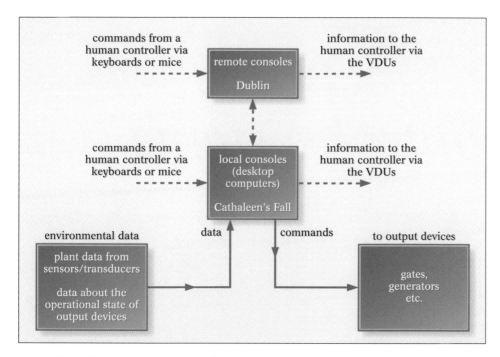

commands from a
human controller via
keyboards or mice

remote consoles

Dublin

information to the
human controller via
the VDUs

commands from a
human controller via
keyboards or mice

local consoles
(desktop
computers)

Cathaleen's Fall

information to the
human controller via
the VDUs

environmental data

data

commands

to output devices

plant data from
sensors/transducers

data about the
operational state of
output devices

gates,
generators
etc.

▲ *A block diagram of the proposed automatic monitoring system to be installed in the Erne system.*

More about ... computer control (repeat commands) pages 35–37.

Why do you think people still form part of the control process?
In your opinion, what is the likelihood that the water control system will become totally automated – replacing the engineers with intelligent machines?

There are many different types of both input and output devices used in the Erne Hydroelectric Development. Make a list of all the output devices you can think of that are used within the system. Describe what each device does.

You should now know about:
- **some aspects of how a hydroelectric power station operates,**
- **environmental, social and economic considerations that need to be taken into**

account when technological projects are undertaken,
- **the monitoring and control that needs to be undertaken in a hydroelectric power station,**
- **representing systems and parts of systems using flow-block diagrams and flow charts,**
- **analysing systems as processes with inputs and outputs,**
- **using systems kits or a computer program to model aspects of control systems.**

You should now be able to complete the task below, which may form part or all of your coursework.
Use a computer control package, together with any sensors and output devices you may need, to develop an integrated monitoring and control system for an environment. The environment could represent:
- some aspect of the Erne development,
- growing large quantities of food in stable conditions,
- a busy railway junction or station,
- office energy management,
- a multi-storey car park,
- a lift in a block of flats.

TASK

Electronic control systems

All the ideas you have met so far in this book can be applied to electronic control systems. In this book, electronic control systems include systems that use either electronics or a computer program (or both) for control. The activities in this chapter will give you a chance to model or mimic fairly simple control systems, so that you can gain some understanding of the ideas met so far.

A temperature control system

One of the easiest of physical conditions to monitor and control is the temperature of an environment. Accurate temperature control is very important in a wide range of situations such as:

- processing food products,
- medical applications – for example, special care baby unit and intensive care,
- growing plants in commercial glasshouses,
- parts of buildings where, for example, there may be temperature-sensitive equipment.

Temperature sensors can be combined with electronic systems to control temperature. In the following activity, you can maintain the temperature inside a model house using both open-loop and closed-loop control.

You will need:
- a 12 V, 24 W lamp to act as a heater,
- a low voltage power supply for the lamp,
- a model house (obtainable from the ASE) or an old shoe box,
- two thermometers: –5 °C to 50 °C (or –10 °C to 100 °C)

Switch on the heater. Measure and record both the inside temperature and the outside temperature (ambient temperature) at regular intervals during the investigation. Record all of your results in a table like this:

Time/ minutes	Inside temperature/ °C	Outside temperature/ °C
0		
1		
2		
3		
...		
13		
14		
15		

On a single piece of graph paper, plot the inside and outside temperatures against time. The investigation could be repeated using extra insulation inside the walls of the house, roof insulation, cavity walls and double glazing.
Explain the shapes of the graphs.
Does this system have any feedback?
Do you think this is a useful heating system? If not, explain why.

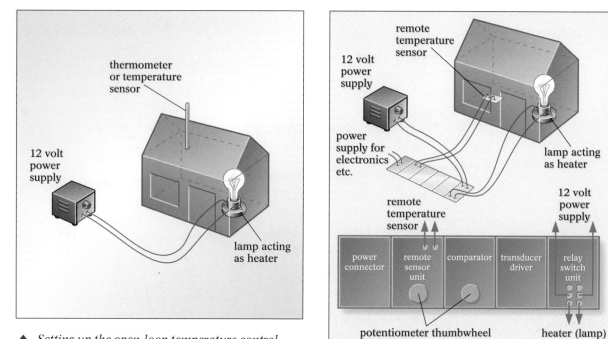

▲ Setting up the open-loop temperature control system.

▲ Setting up the closed-loop temperature control system.

▲ A central heating thermostat.

You will need:
- a 12 V, 24 W lamp to act as a heater,
- a low voltage power supply for the lamp,
- a model house (or an old shoe box),
- two thermometers: −5 °C to 50 °C (or −10 °C to 100 °C).

You will also need the following boards from an electronic systems kit:
- power connector,
- remote temperature sensor,
- remote sensor unit,
- comparator,
- transducer driver,
- relay unit.

Set up the apparatus as shown on page 27 'closed loop temperature control system'.

Switch on the power supply to the relay. Make sure that the lamp switches on and off when the potentiometer on the comparator is turned one way and then the other.

Turn the potentiometer on the sensor unit to the centre position.

Adjust the potentiometer on the comparator until the lamp is just on.

You can now use this potentiometer to set the temperature in your 'house'.

Set the temperature you require for the inside of the house.

Record the inside temperature and the outside temperature (ambient temperature) at regular intervals (for example, every minute) during the investigation.

Record all your results in a table.

On a single piece of graph paper, plot the inside and outside temperatures against time. The investigation could be repeated using extra insulation inside the walls of the house, roof insulation and cavity walls.

Explain the shapes of the graphs.

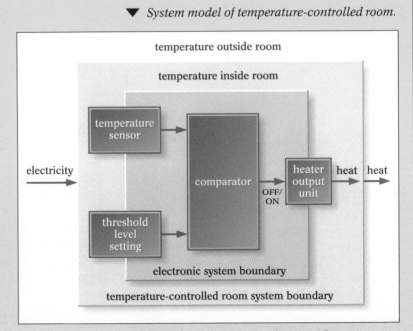

▼ *System model of temperature-controlled room.*

Does this system have any feedback?

What details in the graphs illustrate that this is a closed-loop temperature control system?

Do you think this is a useful heating system? If so, explain why.

Does the position of the internal temperature sensor affect the response of this system?

Try placing the temperature sensor closer to or further away from the source of heat. Compare the graphical results for a series of different positions.

Draw a system diagram for this temperature control system.

> **More about ...** comparators pages 103–104.

> **More about ...** transducer drivers pages 97–98.

> **More about ...** relays page 98.

> **More about ...** home-made temperature sensor and connections into an electronic systems kit *STEP Key stage 3 Datafile*.

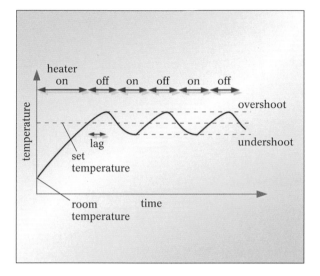

A graph showing the change in room temperature when using an on/off control system.

More about ... hunting and lag page 14.

This temperature controlled system has the heater either fully on or fully off. It is possible to design a system in which the heater output can be varied.

> What are the advantages of being able to adjust the heater output to any value between fully on and fully off?
> When should the rate of heat produced be greatest?
> When should the rate of heat produced be least?

When the room temperature falls below the set temperature, the heater is switched on, but it takes time for the heater to transmit heat into the room. We say there is **lag** between the heater switching on and the room warming up. This means the room temperature falls further below the set temperature (it *undershoots*) before the heater starts to have an effect.

Similarly, when the room temperature rises above the set temperature, the heater switches off. There is lag here, too, because it takes time for the heater to cool down, and for heat to be lost from the room (through the roof, walls, doors and so on). So the room temperature will continue to rise above the set temperature (it *overshoots*) before the cooling starts to have an effect.

These two cases of lag mean that the temperature never settles down but fluctuates about the set temperature. The system is said to be **hunting**. Hunting and lag are natural parts of many control systems.

> What are the problems with this type of temperature control system?
> Suggest a control system where lag would be a major problem.
> Are there control systems where lag is an advantage?

You should now know about:
- **using sensors to monitor temperature,**
- **modelling a temperature control system using feedback,**
- **lag in a system,**
- **hunting in a system.**

You should now be able to complete the task below, which may form part or all of your coursework.

Use an electronic systems kit or other electronic means to model one of the following.
- A smart card used to open a lock.
- A simple keypad used to operate a lift between two floors.
- A system that maintains the humidity level in a tropical greenhouse.
- An automatic sun follower used to collect energy to heat a house hot-water system.

In each case draw your system as a flow-block diagram and identify:
- inputs, processes, and outputs,
- where feedback is used to modify the way the system works,
- where lag has an effect on the system,
- what non-electrical devices or other materials you have integrated within your model.

Computer control systems

The microcomputers that you use in school for control activities will require **interfaces** or buffer boxes.

An interface usually has:

- a power supply system, which powers output devices that are connected to it,
- protection circuitry that ensures devices can be safely connected directly to the interface outputs,
- protection circuitry on the inputs to prevent inappropriate input systems from damaging the microcomputer system.

Many interfaces have a control that permits a choice of output supply voltage – the values are usually 12 V, 9 V, 6 V, 4.5 V, 3 V.

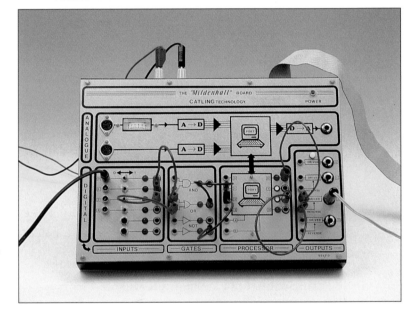

▲ *An interface or buffer box.*

Interfaces have a variety of inputs and outputs. They usually have a number of **binary** (on/off) inputs. Some have *motor-pair outputs*. These are used to allow *bi-directional* (forward and reverse) control of motors rather than just on/off control. Other interfaces may have **analogue** inputs or outputs. Analogue input interfaces (ports) allow us to measure a **signal** (for example temperature or position) using a microcomputer system. Analogue output systems allow us to control output levels (for example the brightness of a lamp or the speed of a motor).

Binary inputs and outputs are usually numbered. For example, an interface may have eight binary inputs; these inputs will be numbered 0 to 7. We say that this set of eight inputs represents an eight-bit binary number; each input represents one *bit* (digit) within the number. A binary input can be either on or off (nothing in between), so we say that 'on' is represented by the number 1, and 'off' by the number 0. So an eight-bit binary number could be 10011100, or perhaps 00110111 (note that we must keep the zeros at the start of a number).

You may have heard the word 'byte' used when talking about computers. A *byte* is another name for an eight-bit binary number.

If we want to convert a byte to a decimal number, we must count in powers of 2. Each bit of the byte tells us whether a particular power of 2 is in the decimal number. For example, if input 3 is 'on' then bit number 3 is set to 1. This means that $2^3 (= 8)$ is in the decimal number; we say that the value represented by bit number 3 is 8. However, if input 3 is 'off', then bit number 3 is set to 0, and 2^3 is not in the decimal number; in this case, we say that bit number 3 is 0.

Powers of 2

A power is really just a way of saying 'write this number down this many times, and multiply your list of numbers together'. For example, '2 to the power 4' means write 2 down 4 times, and multiply. So this is the result:

$$2 \times 2 \times 2 \times 2$$

and the answer is 16.

Rather than write '2 to the power 4', we can write 2^4, and so:

$$2^4 = 2 \times 2 \times 2 \times 2 = 16.$$

Two extra things to remember are that $2^1 = 2$ and $2^0 = 1$.

The decimal number associated with the whole byte (eight-bit binary number) is given by adding the values represented by each bit. For example, 11001001 is equivalent to:

$$(1 \times 2^7) + (1 \times 2^6) + (0 \times 2^5) + (0 \times 2^4) + (1 \times 2^3)$$
$$+ (0 \times 2^2) + (0 \times 2^1) + (1 \times 2^0) = 201$$

Note that bit number 7 is on the left; when writing the byte, we order the bits 7–6–5–4–3–2–1–0. Bit number 7 represents the biggest value ($2^7 = 128$), so we call it the *most significant bit* (msb). And so bit number 0 is the *least significant bit*, since it represents the smallest value ($2^0 = 1$).

Inputs

We use different words to mean the same things with inputs. If an input is switched 'on', it can also be described as 'high' or 'true'. If an input is 'off', then it is also 'low' or 'false'. The table shows how the terms are related.

Input	Other descriptions		Bit
on	high	true	1
off	low	false	0

Some interfaces behave in different ways in response to an input signal. You should always check to see what type of input signal your interface reads as 'on' – it could be when a switch is opened or it could be when a switch is closed!

Outputs

The outputs from interfaces are usually protected. They are capable of controlling devices but *may* not be capable of driving them. This kind of output must be connected to the input of a transducer driver before it can be used to control a device.

More about ... transducer drivers pages 97–98.

▼ *The use of a transducer driver.*

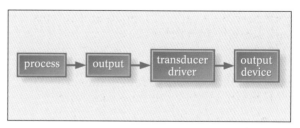

However, the outputs of some interfaces are able to control *and* drive devices such as motors, lamps, solenoids, and relays. The use of interfaces with these devices can model systems quite effectively.

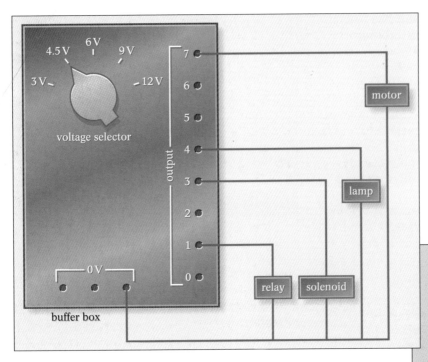

▲ *Outputs from an interface box.*

Computer languages differ in many ways, for example in their **syntax** – the 'words' they use and the way the programs are structured. You will need to refer to the instruction manual for each computer control language to see the correct syntax. The manual should also show you how to enter the language into the computer, and how the computer then uses the language.

When exploring a control language for the first time, it is always useful to have a device or two to control. Connect a number of devices to the computer via the interface or buffer box, and try out some of the activities that follow.

Output devices may be connected to different interfaces in different ways. The diagram shows how loads are attached to some interfaces. You should always check that you understand how to connect the output devices before you start to control them. Some output devices, for example, buzzers and light emitting diodes (LEDs), must be connected a certain way round. It is very important that you connect them the right way round. If you do not, the devices may be damaged.

 Computer software control

The interface uses a set of 'on' and 'off' inputs and outputs to control devices. But the interface is connected to a computer, which 'decides' how to control the devices. To do that, you have to write a *program* in the computer to tell it how you want the device to work. It would be very difficult for you to program the computer using 1s and 0s ('on's and 'off's), so you need to use a *language* that you can understand, and the computer can convert to 1s and 0s.

Immediate command mode

This involves entering commands via the keyboard (or mouse pointer system) to cause device(s) to be turned off or on. For devices connected to lines (outputs) 4 and 7, such commands could be:

```
SWITCH ON LINE 4
SWITCH OFF LINE 7
```

▼ *Flow chart version of the switching commands.*

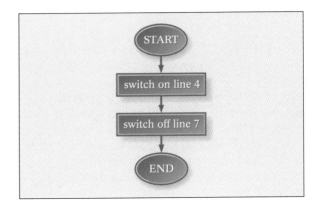

The result of these commands should be that the device connected to line 4 is switched on, and the device connected to line 7 is switched off.

Once a command is executed (carried out), an output line stays in the same state unless you use another command to change it. In the example, line 4 will remain 'on' until you enter a command to switch it 'off'.

Entering a program

Rather than enter 'immediate' commands every time an action is required, it is possible to write a list of commands and enter the list into the microcomputer *memory*. The microcomputer can then be instructed to execute (RUN) the commands in the list (program) in order, just as if you were entering the immediate commands in that sequence.

The method by which you enter the program of commands is different to the method of entering immediate commands. You will need to look at your computer control manual for the language you are using. You can enter a sequence of commands and then instruct the microcomputer to execute the commands in the list. For example:

```
SWITCH ON LINE 1
SWITCH ON LINE 3
SWITCH ON LINE 7
SWITCH OFF LINE 3
SWITCH OFF LINE 7
SWITCH ON LINE 4
SWITCH ON LINE 7
SWITCH OFF LINE 7
SWITCH OFF LINE 1
SWITCH OFF LINE 4
```

The microcomputer will read and execute this list of commands very quickly and return to the immediate command mode or jump out of the program.

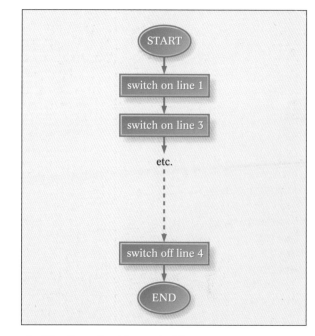

▲ *The flow chart for part of the program.*

Try entering a program like the one on the left, and run it. Watch the output lines very carefully. What do you notice? Can you see them coming on and off?

The program may be executed so quickly that you cannot see the output devices switching on or off. You need to slow the whole program down. You can do this by putting a WAIT or PAUSE command into the program.

Measuring time

To make the computer execute commands at set times from the start of the sequence, you will need to include commands in the program that make the system sense (or count) time.

In many languages, these commands will be WAIT, DELAY or PAUSE commands. You may often see them written as WAIT 10 or PAUSE 20. The number following the command will be the time the microcomputer has to count before proceeding to the next command in the program. The units of time could be milliseconds, centiseconds or seconds. Check your control language manual.

Add WAIT, PAUSE, or equivalent commands between the lines in the previous program. For example:

```
SWITCH ON LINE 1
WAIT 50
SWITCH ON LINE 3
WAIT 230
SWITCH ON LINE 7
SWITCH OFF LINE 3
WAIT 65
SWITCH OFF LINE 7
SWITCH ON LINE 4
WAIT 70
SWITCH ON LINE 7
WAIT 25
SWITCH OFF LINE 7
SWITCH OFF LINE 1
SWITCH OFF LINE 4
```

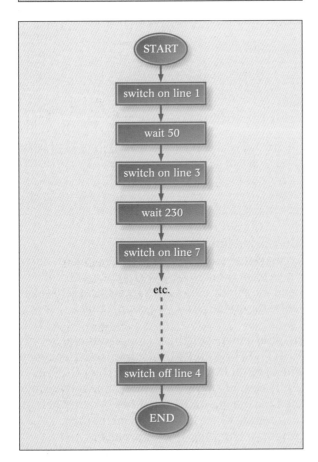

▲ *A flow chart of the 'wait' program.*

Most control languages include a program editor, which allows you to change programs already entered into the computer, rather than having to enter the whole program again.

Bi-directional on/off control

The above commands can be used to switch a motor on and off. You may want to change the direction of the motor. There are several ways of doing this and the method you choose will depend upon the type of computer interface you have.

If you have an interface with individual output lines, one line could operate the motor (on/off) and a second output line could operate a reversing relay (energised/not energised).

> **More about ...** relays page 98.

The relay output causes the relay contacts to move between the upper and lower connections. You will notice that current flows through the motor in different directions, backwards and forwards. The motor output causes the current to flow (or stop flowing) through the motor – so the motor is on (or off).

> Try various combinations of commands to make:
> - the motor run in one direction,
> - the motor run in the reverse direction,
> - the motor switch off.
>
> Connect a buggy (such as a LEGO® buggy) to your computer. Write a control program that will cause the buggy to travel along a preset path from a given stationary position.

Some interfaces have pairs of motor outputs. If you have them, the motor should be connected to one of these pairs.

> If your interface has a motor output pair, try to make the motor run in the reverse direction.

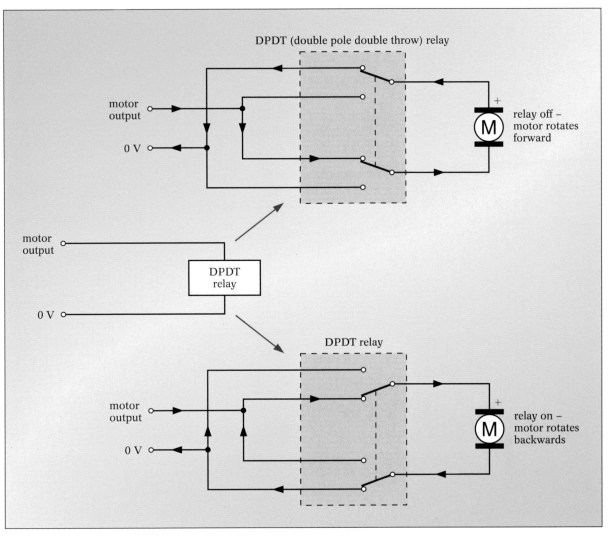

▲ *Connecting a motor and a relay.*

On page 24, we talked about the control of spillway gates in the Erne hydroelectric power station. These gates were raised and lowered by motors.

> Design a spillway gate model that will open and close, and will stop in positions where it is partly open or partly closed. The motor can be operated with a single output line, although this would not allow the motor to be reversed.

Repeating commands within a program

You may need to repeat a sequence of commands over and over again. You could do this by entering a long list of commands that simply repeats a sequence a number of times. However, you could introduce a *loop* into the program, so that the computer returns to the start of the loop when the last command in the loop has been executed. There are two types of loop command, unconditional and conditional.

In an *unconditional loop*, the computer continually returns to the start of the loop and starts again. An example would be a

REPEAT–FOREVER loop. The commands would look like this:

```
REPEAT
SWITCH ON LINE 4
SWITCH OFF LINE 4
FOREVER
```

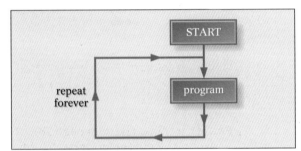

▲ *An unconditional loop.*

This program would execute continuously, and would only end when you stopped the program executing or when you switched off the computer!

> On page 24, we talked about control of a closed-circuit television camera in the Erne Hydroelectric Development. The camera was continuously moved backwards and forwards by a motor.
>
> Try to model this. The program must instruct the camera to scan its viewed area repeatedly, returning to the start position at the end of each scan.

In a *conditional loop*, some condition has to be fulfilled before the computer returns to the start of the loop. An example of a conditional loop is where a program has to execute a command a certain number of times.

A conditional loop may also be used so that something or someone could interrupt the flow of the program and start a new sequence of commands. An example is a REPEAT–UNTIL loop. Here, the commands will be executed until a certain condition is fulfilled. The condition could be:

- a switch is pressed,
- the time is up.

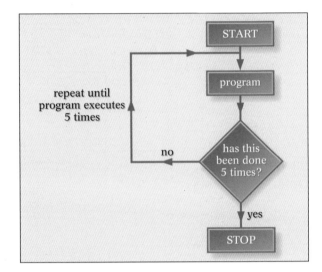

▲ *A conditional loop where the program must execute five times.*

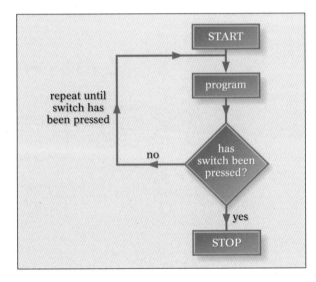

▲ *A conditional loop where a switch stops the program.*

IF–THEN–ELSE–ENDIF

Another way of changing the flow of a computer program is to use the IF–THEN–ELSE–ENDIF structure. This usually looks like:

```
IF condition THEN
    commands
ELSE
    commands
ENDIF
```

- If the condition is true then the commands between the THEN and ELSE statements are executed and those between the ELSE and ENDIF statements are ignored.
- If the condition is false then the commands between the ELSE and ENDIF statements are executed and those between the THEN and ELSE statements are ignored.

This command structure is easier to see as a flow chart. You will probably find that when programs get more complex, it will be easier to draw them as flow charts.

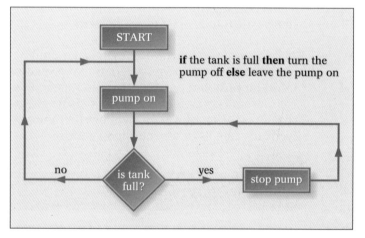

if the tank is full **then** turn the pump off **else** leave the pump on

▲ *Flow chart for IF–THEN–ELSE–ENDIF sequence; the condition is whether the tank is full.*

How can you write a control program that will turn on a motor only if a switch is closed? We will write a program that will do this, and that will also turn off (but turn on a lamp) when the switch is open. The commands to tell the computer to check for an input signal could be something like:

```
INPUT ON? 1
INPUT OFF? 4
```

The first command checks that there is an input on line 1. The second command checks that there is no input on line 4.

The program (flow chart on page 38) you need to control the motor will look something like:

```
REPEAT
    IF INPUT OFF? 3 THEN
        SWITCH ON 7
    ELSE
        SWITCH OFF 7
    ENDIF
    IF INPUT ON? 5 THEN
        SWITCH ON 4
    ELSE
        SWITCH OFF 4
    ENDIF
UNTIL (condition)
```

Sending signals into the computer

So far we have been looking at control programs that send signals out from the computer interface. Most control systems require information or signals from changes in the 'outside world'. You need to know how to send signals into the computer.

Connect a simple switch to the input side of your interface. You should see an LED by the side of the input to show you that a signal is present.

Connect the switch, lamp and motor to the correct input and output lines and make this program work correctly.

Design and model systems to do the following:
- sound an alarm each time a switch is pressed,
- sound an alarm when a switch has been pressed 7 times,
- sound an alarm if a switch has not closed after 10 seconds,
- sound an alarm when a switch has been pressed 7 times, which then stops when a different switch is pressed.

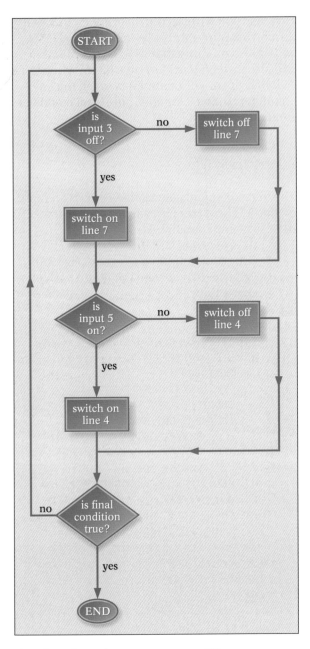

▲ *Flow chart of sequence on page 37.*

Design and model a system to open (and close) a pair of curtains, when a control switch is opened (and closed). The curtains must fully open and stop and fully close and stop. The program must also turn off the motor and sound an alarm if the curtains take too long to either open or close.

Feedback

You will often need to know whether or when something has reached a certain position. This could be, for example, when a door has fully opened, when a lift has reached a certain height, or when a box is present on a conveyor belt.

In the Erne Hydroelectric Development, the control system needs to know the position of the fish pass gates when they are being moved. It is important not to open a fully opened gate, or close a fully closed gate. In these cases *limit switches* are used. These operate when the gates move to the limits of their allowed movement; a signal is sent to the control system to indicate that a gate is fully open or fully closed.

The signals from limit switches are an example of feedback – system *input* signals that provide information about the *output* of the system; this is a closed-loop system. A motor control system that does not employ limit switches (or other feedback signals) is an open-loop control system.

> **More about ...** feedback page 13.

> **More about ...** open- and closed-loop control page 108.

A limit switch is one example of a device that can send signals into a computer interface. There are many analogue devices – light sensors, temperature sensors, magnetic field sensors, rotation sensors and position sensors – that can be used to send signals into the interface. Analogue sensors produce signals that vary continuously. For example, a temperature sensor that measures from 0 °C to 100 °C produces a signal that can represent any value from 0 °C to 100 °C (such as 45.3 °C). A computer can only recognise combinations of binary (on/off) signals. We have to convert the analogue signals into binary signals (also called **digital** signals) for the computer to make use of them. The analogue sensors must be connected to an analogue-to-digital converter (ADC).

More about ... analogue-to-digital converters pages 45–47.

 Procedures

Many programming languages enable you to build up programs from modules. Each of these modules is complete in itself and performs a particular function. These modules are often called **procedures** and are usually given names so that they can be 'called up' by other parts of the program.

The following program could also be a procedure that is part of a bigger program; a good name for the procedure would be PROCLAMP (as in PROCedure LAMP).

```
REPEAT
   IF switch_is_closed THEN
      lamp_ON
   ELSE
      lamp_OFF
   ENDIF
   IF switch_is_open THEN
      motor_ON
   ELSE
      motor_OFF
   ENDIF
FOREVER
```

The use of procedures:

● makes a program more readable and understandable,
● allows you to write a program as a sequence of procedures, where each procedure can be written and tested independently at any time,
● enables you to edit a program more easily.

You can then build procedures within the original procedures (you can 'go down another level') but be careful – you can get into a tangle if you try to make it too sophisticated.

Control programs built from several levels of procedures may run more slowly than programs written with fewer levels of procedures. Each time a procedure is met the computer has to find the procedure, run it and then return to the main program to get on with the next part. This all takes time, although if the computer is fast enough you may not notice any slowing down. On slower computers, you may need to reduce the number of procedures used to allow the program to run fast enough.

 *Constants and variables*

Constants and variables are values stored as part of the computer program. They are referred to by using names or labels.

Constants are values that do not change as the program runs. They are usually set at the beginning of a program and could represent such things as:

● the maximum allowed water level,
● the number of months in a year,
● the diameter of a pound coin, etc.

We give the constants names that show, in a very brief form, what quantities they represent. When we set the values, at the beginning of a program, we use the form:

```
name = (number)
```

For example:

```
months = 12
diameter = 10
maxlevel = 50
minlevel = 15
switch = 1
```

Variables are values that can be changed during the running of the program. They could represent such things as:

- the number of fish counted through the fish pass,
- the actual water level,
- the number of spillway gates open.

Variables can be changed within a program. For instance, if you have developed a computer program to count fish then one command in the program could be:

```
fish = fish + 1
```

This means that the new value of fish becomes equal to the old value of fish, plus 1. This command could be executed every time a sensor detected a fish.

If you were keeping track of how many times part of a program had been executed you might have a line such as:

```
n = n + 1
```

This means that the new value of *n* becomes equal to the old value of *n*, plus 1.

Variables are often used when counting objects or events.

In the Erne Hydroelectric Development, passes are included in the power station design to enable salmon and eels to move past the dam and power station. An automatic fish counter is included in the fish passes (see pages 20–21).

Design and make a system to count objects moving through a water channel. It should display the count continuously until the counter is reset to zero. The objects may be considered to be:
a mainly above the water (floating), or
b totally submerged within the water, or
c a combination of **a** and **b**.

Chose **a**, **b**, or **c** for your design.

Multiple threshold levels

You may need to detect a range of values of some variable. For example, is the temperature of an environment between 10 °C and 40 °C?

A series of IF statements or decisions can be introduced into a program to detect a particular range of numbers or variable values. For example, this program will control a heater output to maintain the temperature in an environment. (The symbol '<' means 'is less than'; '>' means 'is greater than'. So 'temperature <10' means 'temperature is less than 10'.)

```
REPEAT
    IF temp > 10 THEN
        heater_OFF
    ELSE
        heater_ON
    ENDIF
    IF temp > 10 AND temp < 40 THEN
        fan_ON
    ELSE
        fan_OFF
    ENDIF
    IF temp > 40 THEN
        alarm_ON
    ELSE
        alarm_OFF
    ENDIF
FOREVER
```

Describe what the IF program will do as the temperature in the environment changes. Build a model to demonstrate this program in action.

You will notice that this program contains the word AND. This is being used in exactly the same way as the AND logic in electronic system control. You can also use the OR logic function. Computer languages allow you to use a number of logic functions such as NOT and EOR.

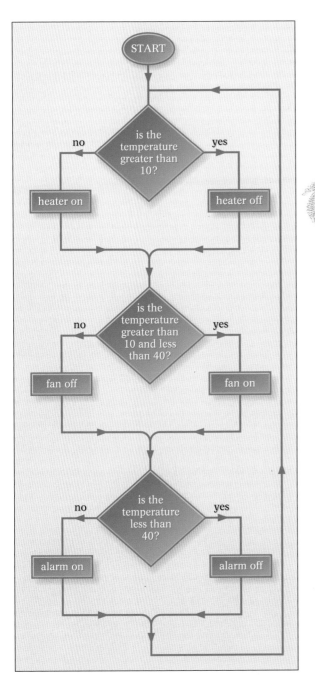

▲ *Flow chart of the IF program.*

More about ... logic functions page 107.

Design and model a system so that if either one of two different switches is pressed, a motor will start up.

Design and model a system so that two switches have to be pressed before a motor will start.

Electronic and computer control systems compared

Some of the examples that you have tried out so far have not been particularly difficult. You might say that using a computer to turn on a lamp is a waste of technology and money! When you are looking at different control contexts you must ask yourself what the best way of solving the problem is. Should you use an electronic system or should you use a computer control system?

For simple, straightforward control it might be better to use a **hard-wired system** (electronic). When the complexity of the control increases, then you should think about using computer control.

Modifying an electronic system may require the system to be physically changed: it will often have to be dismantled, modified, tested and rebuilt before it can be used again. Modifying a *software-based* (computer control) system requires the program held in memory to be modified. The changes to the program can be made away from the environment the program controls: there is no need to dismantle the whole system. It is possible that the changes could be made from some distance away from the system, using a communications network. For example, the programs controlling systems on satellites travelling through the solar system can be modified from ground stations using a radio link. Hard-wired systems on these satellites cannot be mended!

You may notice that when some commands in a computer control program are being executed, nothing else can happen. For example, while executing a WAIT 10 statement the system is just sitting there counting time. No other command in the system is active, and nothing can be detected and acted upon. Another example is that if a signal arrives while the computer is executing a separate procedure, then that signal may be missed. This is different to an electronic system, in which *all* parts of the system are active together and signals can influence the system at any time.

Obviously, the speed at which your computer operates will be the determining factor. You may not notice the pauses or slowing down, or you may be able to put up with them. The computer language may also allow you to program 'interrupts', which may overcome some of these problems.

The solution to a complex control system often lies in a combination of electronic systems with a computer interface, to produce an *integrated control system*.

You should now know about:
- the use of interfaces or buffer boxes,
- writing simple computer control programs,
- the connection of input sensors to a computer,
- the connection of output devices to a computer,
- the use of procedures in computer control programs,
- deciding whether to use computer control or electronics in your projects.

You should now be able to complete the task below, which may form part or all of your coursework.

TASK

An incubator is used by a chicken breeder. Design and model a system that will maintain the temperature inside the incubator to within 1 °C either side of a set temperature.

Decide whether a computer control system, an electronic system, or a mix of these systems is the most appropriate for this application.

Signal conversion

Digital signals

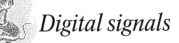

The joystick is an example of a multi-way switch. It provides a number of **digital signals** (binary signals). These digital signals can be sent into an electronic system or into a computer through an interface. When the joystick is in its centre position there is no link between the centre connection and any of the four side connections. The joystick is spring-loaded to return to the centre position when released.

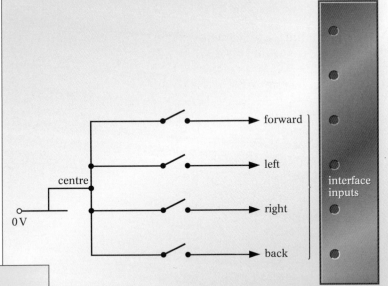

▲ *Connections from a joystick.*

If the joystick is moved to the right, the centre connection touches the right connection. A similar thing happens for movements forward, back and left. Any one of four signals will be produced.

If the joystick is moved up and left at the same time, the centre connection touches the forward and left connections together (and similarly for the other corners). Now a combination (pair) of signals will be produced.

> How many pairs of signals can be produced by the joystick?
> How many different signals in total can be produced by the joystick?

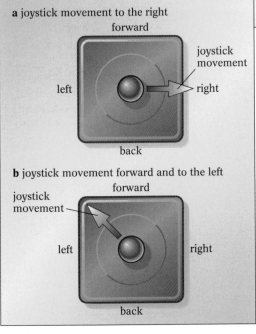

▲ *Joystick movements.*

If you do not have access to a joystick then two DPDT (double pole double throw) switches with centre-off positions will perform the same functions as a joystick.

The forward, back, left and right connections may be used as four digital inputs to an interface. The centre connection of the joystick would be connected to the common line, 0 V.

Look back to page 24 and the description of the CCTV camera used in the Erne Hydroelectric Development. The camera is controlled by two motors with two gearboxes. One motor rotates the camera clockwise and anticlockwise, the other motor rotates the camera up and down.

Design and make a system that uses a joystick to control the position of the camera.
What will be the limits of movement of the camera in each direction? You will have to ensure that the camera does not attempt to move outside these limits. What will you use to detect if the camera has reached the limit of its movement?

Decide whether a computer software system, a hard-wired system or a mix of these systems is the most appropriate for this application.

Are there any other technologies that could be considered for use in this control system, for example hydraulics or pneumatics?

Analogue signals to digital input lines

Many conditions that we need to detect and use in systems are not just 'on' or 'off'. Temperature, light intensity, position, flow rate, volume, and so on may vary within a wide range, so that digital (on/off) sensors are not suitable. Sensors monitoring these conditions produce **analogue signals**. These sensors may be used with a **comparator** to produce digital signals from an analogue source. The comparator acts as a 1-bit **analogue-to-digital converter** (ADC).

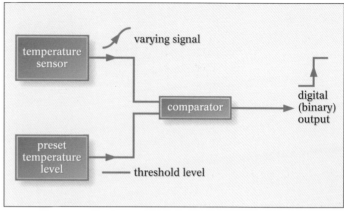

▲ *Comparator system.*

Such a sensor could be used as part of a controller for a temperature control system. You may have used one already.

More about … comparators pages 104–105.

More about … temperature control system pages 26–29.

In the example of the room temperature controller on page 28, if the switching temperature is 25 °C and the temperature falls below 25 °C the heater will come on. Then if the temperature rises slightly above 25 °C the heater will switch off; if it then falls below 25 °C it will switch on again. The system would **oscillate**, switching the heater off, then on, then off, and so on, in quick succession. This is known as **hunting**. The sensed temperature differences could simply be due to small random errors (**noise**) in the temperature sensing system. Two switching levels can be used to avoid hunting due to this noise. One switching level could be set to 26 °C for rising temperature; the second switching level could be set to 24 °C for falling temperature. If the temperature falls to 24 °C, the heater switches on, but the heater would not switch off until the temperature had risen to 26 °C, and vice-versa. Systems that use different switching levels in this way are said to display **hysteresis**. (See figure overleaf.)

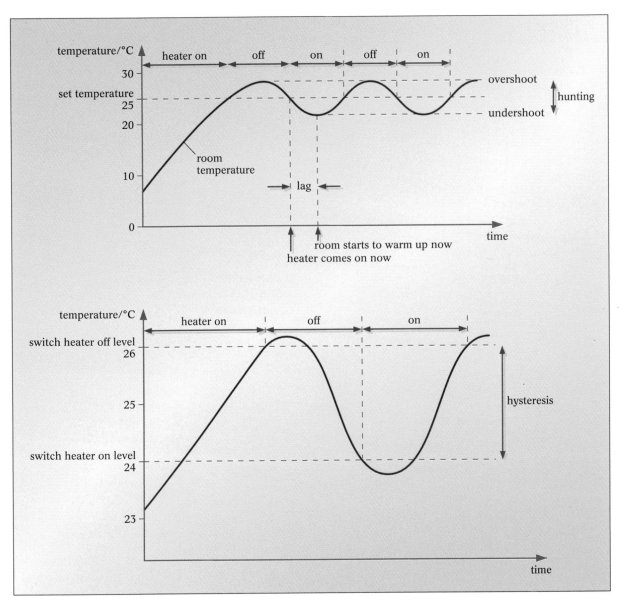

▲ *Hunting and hysteresis.*

Multiple threshold levels

We have talked about how to produce a digital signal for one specific level of an analogue signal, using a comparator. You may want to know when several different specific levels or quantities of signals have been reached. These are known as *multiple threshold levels*.

You can detect multiple threshold levels by using a number of comparators. For instance, two comparators are used to monitor the maximum and minimum temperatures allowed within an environment. When the temperature drops below the minimum value or rises above the maximum value, a comparator changes its signal and the control system can operate an output.

Suppose you want to detect when the level of water in a reservoir has reached any one of five preset levels. You also want to know whether the water level is rising or falling. Design and make a system to do this.

Decide whether a computer software system, a hard-wired system or a mix of these systems is the most appropriate for this application.

More about … monitoring temperatures in an environment pages 26–29.

You can also convert an analogue signal into a many-valued digital signal using a *multi-bit* analogue-to-digital converter. This converts a continuously varying signal into a series of numbered steps. A 4-bit ADC will produce 16 different input values (often this may be enough). An 8-bit ADC is more sensitive, and will produce 256 different input values.

The eight signal lines from an 8-bit ADC must be connected to the eight binary input lines of the interface in the correct order.

More about … input lines of interfaces page 37.

If your interface does not have an internal ADC, then the computer can be instructed to read the value from external ADC, by using a command within a program. If you use an 8-bit ADC, the value read will be between 0 and 255.

The command for reading a value from an ADC is different for different computer languages. Examples include:

```
IN (temp)
```

Here, temp is a variable and will take the value of the ADC signal fed to the input port.

```
temperature = PORT 1
```

Here, temperature is a variable, and the command PORT 1 instructs the computer to get the value of the ADC signal at input port 1.

Many computer systems include an analogue port or 'games' port. This is an input to the computer that provides access to an ADC within the computer. This removes the need to use any ADC circuitry before connecting the sensor to the interface. Some more modern interfaces come with an external ADC, for use when the computer system does not have its own internal ADC.

A computer system with an internal ADC may use commands such as ADVAL (i.e. the Analogue-to-Digital converter VALue). For example:

```
N = ADVAL(1)
```

This will set the variable N to the value of analogue port 1.

You may still need to convert the ADC number into a recognisable measure. For example, the number generated by the ADC may represent a specific temperature in °C, or it may just be a number on a scale that needs *calibrating*, so that you know what each number from the ADC represents on a °C scale.

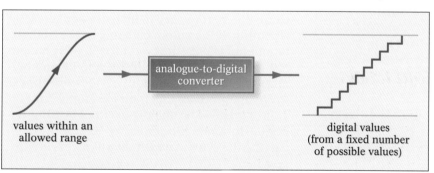

values within an allowed range

digital values (from a fixed number of possible values)

▲ *The function of an analogue-to-digital converter.*

Calibrate the ADC values within the control program.

Is it always necessary to calibrate an analogue sensor? Do you need to know the absolute value, for example 25 °C, or will a number representing this value be sufficient?

Design and make at least one of the following sensors:

- humidity,
- light level,
- rainfall,
- wind speed,
- wind direction,
- vertical position.

They do not have to be sensors that have an analogue output – they could provide a multi-level output similar to that of the ADC, or a pulse output (which could be an up/down counter or supply an on/off output).

Design and make a system that uses a sensor to monitor the level of a condition (rainfall, for example) that it senses. Your system must display this level in two different units: for example, the level of rainfall could be displayed in either millimetres or inches. You should be able to change the units by using a two-position switch. The system should sound different alarms if the level goes above or below preset levels.

Design and model a system to control the environment inside a glasshouse, such that the light level, air temperature, soil temperature, air humidity, soil moisture content and ventilation will be maintained at preset levels.

More about ... environmental control in a glasshouse pages 26–29, 70–71.

The Erne Hydroelectric Development control room takes inputs from remote sensors that monitor humidity, temperature, rainfall, wind speed, wind direction and water level. Design and model sensors that will detect a range of these conditions.

You will need to think about:

- what sensors you need,
- whether each sensor is analogue or digital,
- whether analogue signals should be converted into digital signals,
- whether analogue signals are large enough or should be amplified,
- whether analogue signals are within ranges that can be monitored,
- what decisions will be made once a signal has been measured,
- whether the signal should be compared to a preset value.

You may want to use a VDU to display the values of the signals being sent into the computer. You could compare these signals to one or more threshold levels.

Analogue output

The output devices we have looked at so far have been controlled as on/off (two-state) devices. It is also possible to control output devices so that the level of output is somewhere between off and on.

For example, if a motor is used as the output device, a continuously varying output would cause the motor speed to increase or decrease smoothly. If the output can only have a certain number of values, the motor speed will change in a more sudden way. However, if the number of values is large, the output devices will appear to change gradually. Computer systems can approximate to an analogue output by using a **digital-to-analogue converter** (DAC), or by varying the rates at which output pulses are sent out.

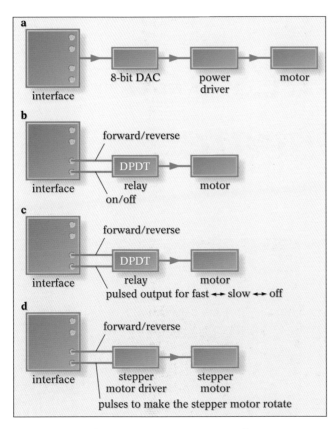

▲ *Methods of connecting a motor to continuous and stepped outputs.*

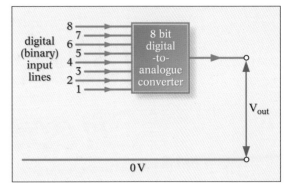

▲ *A block diagram of an 8-bit DAC.*

With an 8-bit DAC, 256 output levels are possible. This is often more than enough levels, so that anyone using an output device will not notice any sudden changes in the output.

You should now be able to complete one of the tasks below, which may form part or all of your coursework.

Design and model a system that will operate a fan, in such a away that the speed of the fan is determined by which of four switches was closed last. The switches have the following functions: stop, slow, medium and fast, and should be sprung to return to the open state when released. If two or more switches are pressed at the same time then they should be ignored. You could use a centre-off joystick to do this or two DPDT switches with centre-off positions.

Design and model a system that will maintain the light intensity in an environment at a constant level. If the natural light level decreases then the artificial light level must increase, and vice versa.

Power amplification

The output from many digital-to-analogue converter systems is in the form of a low-voltage signal that cannot drive output devices directly. *Power amplification* is required to drive most devices.

You should now know about:
- **the use of analogue sensors with a comparator to provide the equivalent of a digital sensor,**
- **analogue-to-digital converters,**
- **digital-to-analogue converters.**

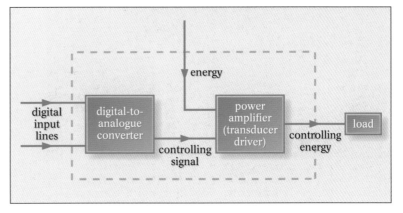

▲ *DAC with power amplifier connected to output device.*

Electronics and healthcare

There are many applications of electronic systems in healthcare. Electronic devices are used for monitoring the condition of a patient and to assist with diagnosis. Electronics has also helped with the development of instruments for treating patients. One of the key features of instruments used in healthcare is that they should have as little effect on the patient as possible – they should be *non-intrusive*. Wherever possible, it is better to monitor the patient's condition without inserting instruments into their body. These photographs show four important areas where electronic instruments are used.

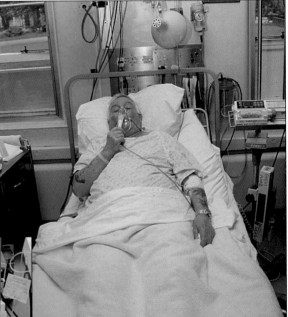

▲ *Intensive care unit (ICU). The medical team in the intensive care unit rely on electronic systems to monitor a patient's condition. If the body's 'measurable quantities' – breathing, pulse-rate, body temperature, blood pressure and blood composition – go above or below certain levels, the medical team will take the necessary action.*

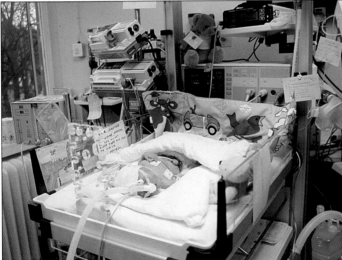

▲ *Special care baby unit (SCBU). Premature babies may be too small for their body functions to carry on normally. If so, the baby must be monitored constantly, usually by checking temperature, pulse-rate and breathing.*

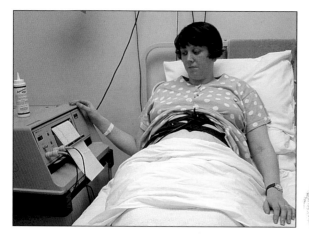

▲ *Foetal heart monitoring. The health of a baby can be checked even when it is still inside the womb.*

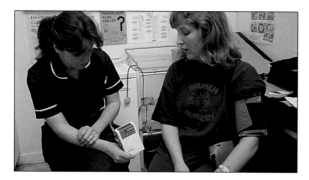

▲ *Checking a patient's blood pressure.*

These systems only *monitor* the patient's condition – they do not *control* it.

Why is it important to make regular measurements of a patient's condition?
How do you think electronics can help doctors and nurses to do this?
Identify the electronic devices used in each photograph.

All of these electronic systems have input, process and output stages. Try to identify the input sensors and the output transducers in the photographs.

Why is it important that the input sensors and output transducers should be selected carefully?
What criteria should be used to select the best sensors and transducers?

More about ... input, process and output page 6.

More about ... sensors and transducers pages 90–101.

The Hewlett-Packard component monitoring system

The more doctors know about a patient's condition, and the sooner they get this information, the greater the chance they have of improving the patient's condition. The Hewlett-Packard component monitoring system is designed to provide accurate, reliable and complete information about the patient. It collects all of the information together and can display it on colour monitors.

The monitoring system is made up of a number of electronic modules. These can be put together to meet the needs of hospitals, doctors and patients. It covers all aspects of hospital procedures, from routine examinations to specialised intensive care applications.

The set of electronic modules covers functions such as:

- pulse-rate monitor,
- electrocardiograph (ECG) used to monitor the heart,
- combined ECG and respiration (breathing) monitor,
- blood pressure monitor,
- cardiac (heart) output monitor,
- sensors for carbon dioxide and oxygen levels in the blood.

Inputs from other devices such as ventilators and gas analysers can also be processed. All of the information can be passed to the Recorder module and to a variety of printers and chart recorders.

> What are the advantages to the medical staff of this integrated system?
> How does this help with caring for the patient?

Designing systems for use in hospitals

There are a number of issues to be considered when designing any equipment for use in hospitals. Some of the issues considered by Hewlett-Packard are given below.

1 The need for the system to be **fail-safe** – if anything goes wrong with the system, for example an electrical power failure, it should automatically provide a warning or switch to a back-up system.

> What do you think fail-safe means?
> Why is fail-safe so important in medical applications?

2 The need for cleanliness and sterile conditions – the equipment must be designed so that it can be thoroughly cleaned or sterilised so there is no risk of the patient being infected.

3 Staff in hospitals often have to move very quickly – sometimes in life-or-death situations – so any equipment used should be easily moved and should not get in the way.

4 Patient confidence – people in hospital are under stress and are concerned about their health. Any equipment used should help to reduce a patient's concerns, not add to them.

> Explain how the Hewlett-Packard system meets these design requirements.

Before the design of the system was finalised, prototypes were put into hospitals as part of a series of field trials. Here are some of the views of doctors and nurses as a result of these trials.

> *'The system provides a complete picture of each patient.'*
>
> *'It is much easier and quicker to assess the patient's condition because all of the information is in one place – this also allows us to reassure the patient about their condition.'*
>
> *'The system is very flexible, allowing us to target individual patient's needs.'*

Keeping a check on patients

The Hewlett-Packard component monitoring system can provide a printed record of the patient's temperature, blood pressure and pulse-rate. These are measured and recorded at regular intervals and help to show whether the body is working normally.

> Look at the chart on page 53 and answer the following questions.
>
> Can you see a link between the temperature and pulse-rate of the patient?
> Describe what you see happening.
>
> A healthy patient's temperature will vary slightly. Why do you think this happens?
> Find out what is an acceptable range above and below normal body temperature for a healthy person.
>
> Pulse-rates also vary in healthy people. What causes the pulse-rate to change?

You will notice that two readings for blood pressure are recorded – systolic and diastolic. The systolic pressure – the higher reading – is when the heart contracts, the diastolic pressure – the lower reading – is when the heart relaxes. The systolic blood pressure shows whether the heart is pumping properly. It is also important to check that the heart is relaxing properly; this is shown by the diastolic blood pressure.

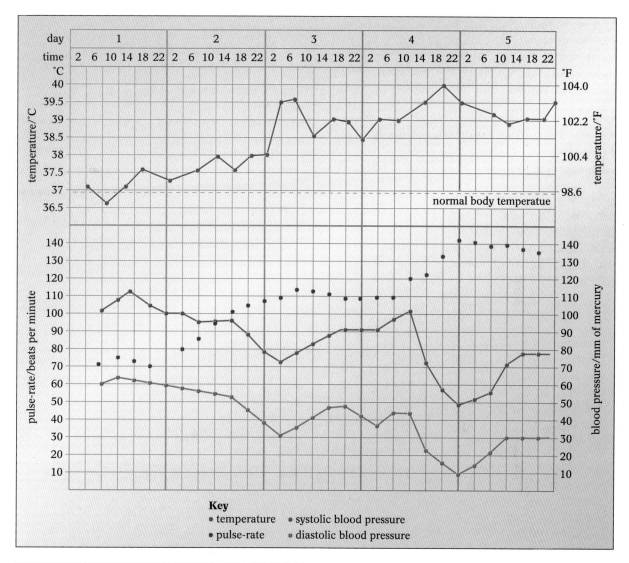

Key
- temperature
- systolic blood pressure
- pulse-rate
- diastolic blood pressure

▲ *Chart showing temperature, blood pressure and pulse-rate.*

Why do you think it is important to measure and record both blood pressure readings?
Can you see a pattern that links the temperature, blood temperature and pulse-rate for this patient? Explain the pattern in your own words.

Taking routine measurements

If the patient is not in intensive care, temperature, blood pressure and pulse-rate measurements are usually taken using non-electronic devices. However, all of these and other quantities can be measured and monitored electronically.

What are the advantages of using electronics? What are the disadvantages of using electronics?

Some things to consider:
- when the measurements need to be taken,
- how often they need to be taken,
- whether they need to be made continuously,
- the importance of the personal touch that can be provided by nurses and other medical staff.

The use of both electronic devices and nursing care to monitor a patient's progress allows maximum flexibility in meeting the needs of the patient. This helps medical staff plan the best course of treatment for their patients.

Monitoring mothers and babies during pregnancy

During pregnancy, the condition of an unborn baby can be monitored by checking on the performance of its heart. This is known as foetal heart monitoring. Nurses and doctors can listen to the heart using a hand-held, trumpet-like device called a foetal stethoscope. However, an electronic ultrasound machine can also be used to monitor the heart.

> **More about ...** ultrasonics page 60.

> Examine the chart. Is it clear to you what the readings mean? Can you interpret the readings?

The Hewlett-Packard component monitoring system provides benefits to both hospital staff and expectant mothers. Parents can find it very reassuring to be able to see a trace of their baby's heartbeat. It is also an easy way for hospital staff to keep an eye on the unborn baby.

> Would you agree that a great deal of training is needed to interpret the readings on the chart? What could be the effects of misreading the information in the charts?

The results can be displayed on a chart printed out by the machine. The mother can start the machine recording when the baby (foetus) gives a kick or when she feels a contraction. The chart can be compared with the foetal heart reading. The Hewlett-Packard system also records the mother's heart rate, and this can be displayed alongside the baby's.

> Explain the advantages of this electronic system over the non-electronic devices, both for the expectant mother and for the medical staff.

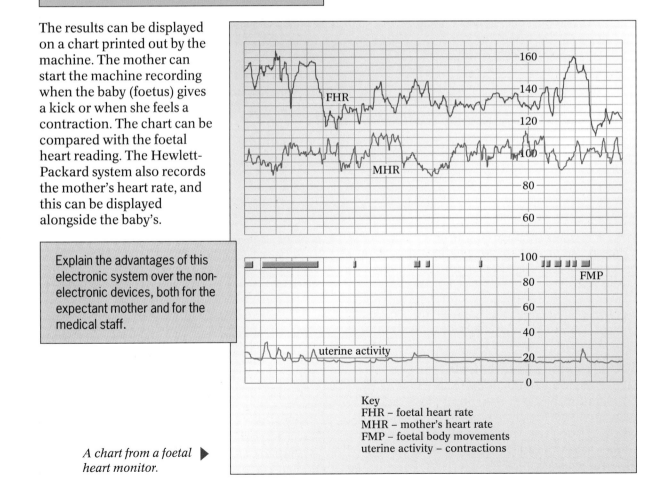

Key
FHR – foetal heart rate
MHR – mother's heart rate
FMP – foetal body movements
uterine activity – contractions

A chart from a foetal ▶
heart monitor.

Investigating electronic systems in healthcare

Circuit diagrams are provided for all the systems investigated here. However, most of the systems can be made or modelled first using an electronics systems kit. You may need to build some of the sub-systems using a prototype board or similar board supplied with your kit.

An electronic thermometer

A flow-block diagram showing the sub-systems for an electronic thermometer might look like this.

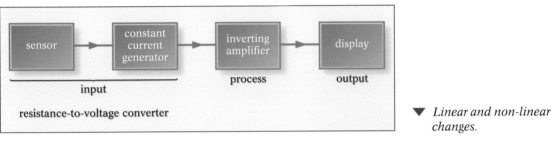

▲ A flow-block diagram for an electronic thermometer.

The input stage

One type of sensor used to detect temperature changes is called a *thermistor*. The electrical resistance of a thermistor changes as the temperature changes. These changes in resistance cause changes in the potential difference (voltage) across the thermistor. The thermistor can be used in a potential divider sub-system.

More about ... resistance and potential difference page 90.

More about ... potential dividers page 91.

More about ... thermistors page 92.

One problem with a thermistor is that the changes in resistance with temperature are not *linear*. This means that equal changes in temperature do not give equal changes in potential difference. This makes the thermometer difficult to calibrate.

To make a linear thermometer, a *diode* is used as the sensor. If the electrical current through the diode is kept constant, the resistance of the diode, and hence the voltage across it, drops as the temperature increases. This is an example of a resistance-to-voltage converter.

▼ *Linear and non-linear changes.*

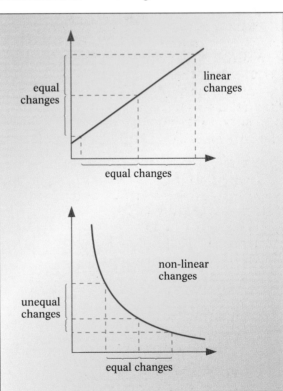

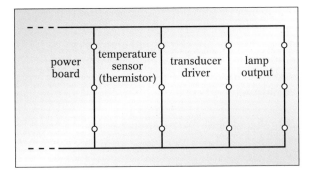

▲ *A thermometer circuit based on the thermistor.*

Build the thermometer circuit above using an electronic systems kit.
Make sure that as the temperature increases, the lamp glows more brightly.
Replace the temperature sensor board with a remote sensor. Make sure that the system still works.
Now replace the lamp with a 0–5 V voltmeter. Calibrate the voltmeter with a range of temperatures: 0 °C, 50 °C and 100 °C.
Try measuring temperatures with this electronic thermometer.

Build the input and initial processing stage of the electronic thermometer below on a prototype board. The constant current needed by the diode can be provided by using an **operational amplifier** (op-amp) as a constant-current generator.

Use a multimeter to measure the voltage V_{out} for a range of temperatures. (You may want to add extra leads to the diode so that you can place it in different environments.)
Plot your results on a graph.

More about ... operational amplifiers pages 103–106.

More about ... constant-current generators page 106.

More about ... multimeters page 88.

▼ *The circuit for the complete electronic thermometer using a diode.*

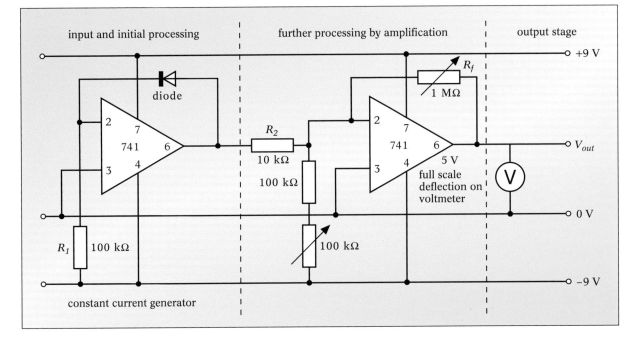

Build the further processing stage of the electronic thermometer.
This involves another op-amp, but this time it is used as an inverting amplifier.

Add this to the first stage you have already built on the prototype board.
Set the potentiometer to about the mid-point.
Connect a multimeter (set to the d.c. 5 V range) to the output.
Change the temperature by holding the diode in your hand.

What happens to the output voltage?
How does this compare with the changes in voltage you measured at the input stage?
Why do you think this is called an inverting amplifier?

More about ... inverting amplifiers page 106.

The amplification factor, or voltage gain, of the amplifier is given by the ratio R_f/R_2. The value of R_f can be changed to make the thermometer suitable for different temperature ranges.

Calculating the temperature range

Here is an example to show you how to calculate the temperature range for your thermometer.

The output voltage change of the first stage should be 2 mV per °C.
If R_f is set to 1 MΩ and R_2 is 10 kΩ, the gain (amplification) should be 100.
The output voltage change per °C should therefore be
100 x 2 mV = 200 mV = 0.2 V
If a 5 V meter is used, a temperature range of 25 °C can be measured.

The output stage

Calibrating your electronic thermometer

What temperature range do you need?
What values of R_f and R_2 should you use?

Use a meter that reads from 0 to 5 volts as the output display.
The thermometer is easy to calibrate because it is linear. You only need to take two readings, say 0 °C and 50 °C. However, it is better to take one or two more to check the linearity.

A summary of the complete circuit
- The input stage uses a diode to detect temperature changes and produce corresponding changes in voltage.
- The constant-current generator provides the constant current needed by the diode.
- The changes in voltage produced by the diode are very small, about 2 mV for every °C. The amplifier increases the size of these voltage changes so that they can be seen on a meter.

You may now want to produce a printed circuit board of the complete themometer.

More about ... producing printed circuit boards pages 82–84.

An electronic pulse-rate meter
When you hold a bright light to your hand, some light passes through. As your heart beats and pushes the blood through your hand, the intensity (amount) of light passing through changes. Your eyes are not sensitive enough to see these changes in light intensity. However, an electronic pulse-rate meter is sensitive enough to detect these changes, and the meter counts the number of changes to give the pulse-rate.

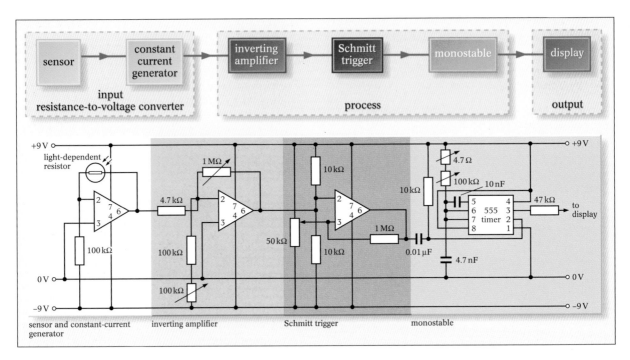

▲ *A flow-block diagram and the circuit for an electronic pulse-rate meter.*

The input stage

This is very similar to the input and initial processing stage of the electronic thermometer – see page 55. The diode has been replaced by a photocell. The photocell detects the very small changes in light intensity that occur with each heartbeat. The electrical resistance of the photocell decreases as more light shines on it. The change in resistance with each beat is about 100Ω. The input stage acts as a resistance-to-voltage converter. These changes in voltage can then be processed by the next stage of the circuit.

Build the input stage of the pulse-rate meter on prototype board.
Connect an oscilloscope across the output terminals of the input stage. Set the gain to about 20 mV/cm and the sweep rate (timebase) to about 20 ms/cm.
Shine a light through your thumb and place your thumb over the photocell.
Look for vertical changes in the way the spot or trace moves across the CRO screen.
Try to estimate the change in voltage.

More about ... cathode-ray oscilloscopes page 88.

The amplifier stage

The output voltage from the input stage should change by about 10 mV every pulse. You can use an op-amp as an inverting amplifier on this output, in the same way as in the electronic thermometer.

More about ... operational amplifiers pages 103–106.

More about ... inverting amplifiers page 106.

Build this stage on the prototype board and add this to your existing circuit.

Use a cathode-ray oscilloscope to measure the changes in the output voltage from the inverting amplifier.

The Schmitt trigger

The analogue signal has to be changed into a digital signal for the counter. This can be done using a **Schmitt trigger**, which is an electrical circuit that 'cleans up' electronic signals. It can be used to turn signals of an uneven shape into pulse-shaped signals.

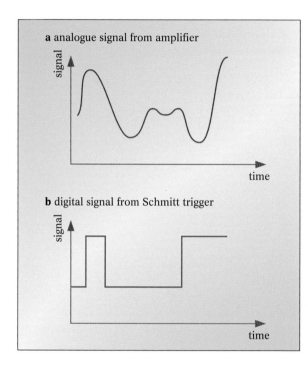

a analogue signal from amplifier

signal

time

b digital signal from Schmitt trigger

signal

time

▲ *Analogue and digital signals. The input to the Schmitt trigger is an analogue signal, the output is a digital signal.*

Connect the Schmitt trigger to the circuit you have constructed so far.
Connect a multimeter (set to the d.c. 5 V range) to the output.
Adjust the 50 kΩ potentiometer until, on each pulse, the multimeter changes sharply from negative to positive.
You could use an oscilloscope to look at the output from the Schmitt trigger.

The signals from the Schmitt trigger may not all be the same. Some of the digital signals may last longer than others. Ideally, all these signals should be of equal length. An electronic sub-system called a **monostable** will convert pulses of different lengths into pulses that all have the same length.

More about ... the monostable page 102.

The monostable you will use is based on a 555 timer.

More about ... the 555 timer pages 102–103.

Build the monostable circuit on your prototype board. Connect the signals from the Schmitt trigger to the monostable input.

The monostable can be used to turn the output from the Schmitt into a series of regular pulses.

Use the Schmitt trigger with monostable to make an LED (light-emitting diode) flash every pulse, to provide the basis for a simple pulse counter. Develop this circuit by adding counting and display sub-systems after the monostable sub-system.

The complete system could be developed further so that it counts pulses for one minute, then pauses for a while, and then resets itself to zero and starts to count again.

Model this part of the system using an electronic systems kit before producing a final, complete circuit for production.

A summary of the complete circuit
- The flow of blood alters the way in which parts of the body transmit light.
- The input stage uses a photocell to detect changes in light intensity.
- The changes in electrical resistance of the photocell are converted into very small voltage signals.
- The amplifier increases the size of these signals.

- The Schmitt trigger turns these signals into digital pulses to operate the monostable.
- The monostable produces a series of regular pulses that matches the heartbeat.

Using ultrasound

The technique called ultrasound is often used in medical applications to produce pictures of the inside of the body. One application is to look at the development of a baby inside the mother's womb. Ultrasound uses frequencies that are too high for the human ear to hear.

> Make an ultrasonic transmitter using the 555 timer circuit shown on the right.

> **More about ...** the 555 timer pages 102–103.

> **More about ...** the astable page 103.

▼ *Ultrasonic receiver circuit.*

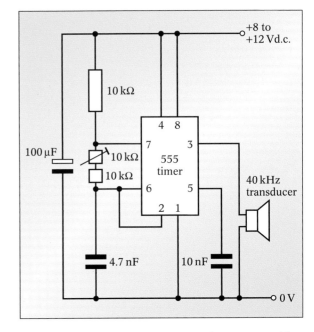

▲ *Ultrasonic transmitter circuit. This is an astable circuit.*

The receiver circuit is more complicated. The relay is energised when it receives a signal from the transmitter. This can be used to switch on a lamp, a motor or another device.

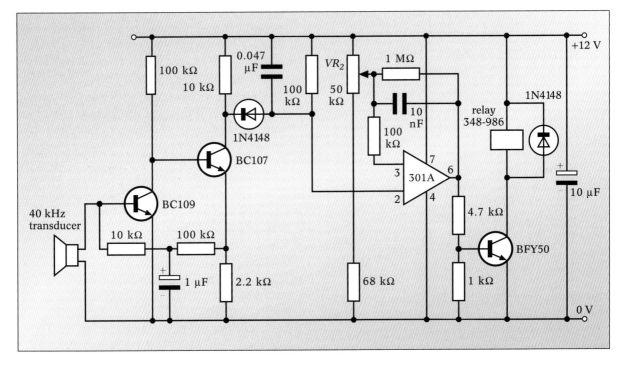

Build the circuit shown at the bottom of page 60. To tune the transmitter and receiver, adjust VR_1 on the transmitter and VR_2 on the receiver to obtain maximum sensitivity. Use an oscilloscope to look at the different signals.

You can use the transmitter and receiver combination to investigate some aspects of the uses of ultrasound in medicine. For example, you could:
- find out how far the signal travels,
- reflect the signal through different angles and off different surfaces,
- find out how far the ultrasound penetrates through different materials and different thicknesses of material.

Ultrasound can also be used in non-medical applications. It can be used instead of visible light or infrared beams in security devices.

Use the transmitter and receiver circuits to make a prototype security system that could be used either:
- to protect a valuable object on display in a museum or shop, or
- in a room at home.

You can also use the circuits to make a remote control device, which could turn on a motor or an electrical appliance.

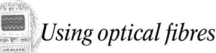

Using optical fibres

Instruments that make use of **optical fibres** allow doctors to look inside the body without making large incisions (cuts), because optical fibres transmit light even when they are bent. A device such as an *endoscope*, which contains optical fibres, can be used to investigate 'inaccessible' areas of the body (for example, the intestines) without any incisions being made.

Here are the flow-block diagrams of a number of systems that use optical fibres to transmit signals or information.

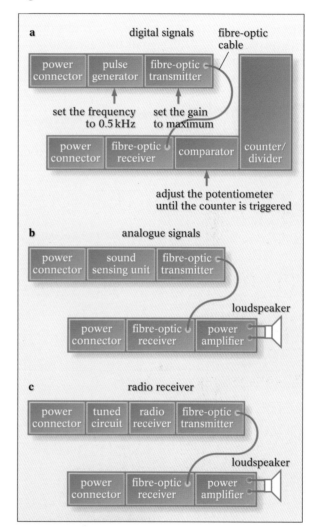

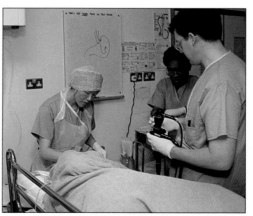

▲ **a** *Investigating the transmission of digital signals.*
b *Investigating the transmission of analogue signals.*
c *Using a radio receiver.*

◀ *An endoscope.*

Build the systems on page 61 using an electronic systems kit, and investigate their uses.

There are a number of very simple circuits that can be used to transmit signals through and receive signals from optical fibres. Two are shown below.

Build these circuits on prototype board and investigate their uses. For some of them you may need to add other sub-systems (such as amplifiers) to process the signal.

You could investigate the effect of:
- changing the length of the optical fibre,
- bending the optical fibre,
- changing the temperature of the fibre (within reasonable limits!),
- putting the fibre under *tensile stress* (stretching it a bit!).

What are the effects on the strength and 'accuracy' of the signal received?
Are the effects the same for analogue and digital signals?

You should now know about:
- **some uses of electronics in healthcare,**
- **building electronic products from given circuits,**
- **the use of thermistors, potential dividers, diodes, operational amplifiers and Schmitt triggers,**
- **ultrasound,**
- **optical fibres,**
- **the use of cathode-ray oscilloscope and a digital multimeter,**
- **developing an electronics project.**

You should now be able to complete one of the tasks opposite, which may form part or all of your coursework.

Whichever situation you decide to investigate, you should research the situation thoroughly. Decide whether hard-wired electronic control, computer control or a mixture of these will provide the best solution.

▼ **a** *Transmitting an analogue signal.*
  b *Transmitting a digital signal.*

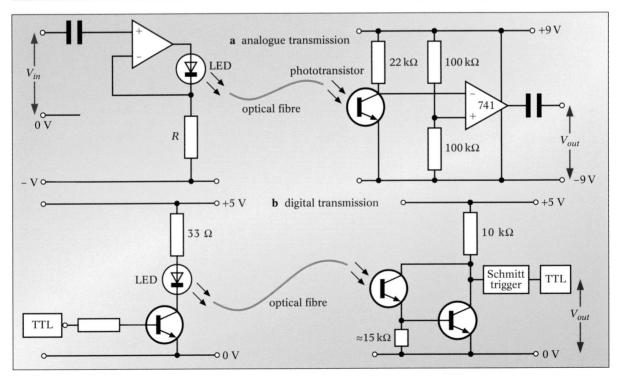

1 Too much exercise too soon could be dangerous for some people. They need to keep a check on their heart-rate. Design and make a fitness monitor that could be used by a wide range of people. It will need to be tough to withstand a lot of physical exercise!

2 The tried and tested method for checking the temperature of a baby's bath water is to put your elbow in the water. Design and make an electronic 'elbow'.

3 The temperature of baby's milk is usually tested by pouring some onto the inside of your wrist or the back of your hand. Design and make an electronic thermometer that indicates if the milk temperature is within acceptable limits. Remember that you may need to sterilise parts of the system each time before it is used.

4 This activity should be carried out under supervision by your teacher.

An electrocardiograph (ECG) is used to monitor the electrical signals produced by the heart. This can be used to provide information about how the heart is working. *Electrodes* are placed on the patient's body to detect the electrical signals, which are very small. There is also a lot of electrical noise produced by the electronic circuitry. It is very difficult to find the signal and tell it apart from the noise. It is rather like listening for the song of a bird on a windy day in a forest.

The circuit suggested below is based on an op-amp but functions as a differential amplifier. In this way, the electrical signal from the heart is amplified and the background noise is cut out. Another op-amp can be connected to the output from the differential amplifier, to amplify the 'cleaned' signal.

Hold one of the electrodes in your hand. Look at the display on the oscilloscope. Now pick up the other electrode with your other hand, so you are holding both electrodes. What happens to the display on the oscilloscope?

Connect the heart monitor to a 'patient'. What happens to the heart-rate if the 'patient' exercises?

 The circuit must be powered by a battery.

5 Design and make a complete electronic fitness package that will provide information about heart-rate, body temperature, breathing rate and any other information that a fitness fanatic might need.

More about ... product development pages 76–79.

More about ... making electronic products pages 82–86.

More about ... analysing control situations pages 80–81.

▼ *A heart monitor.*

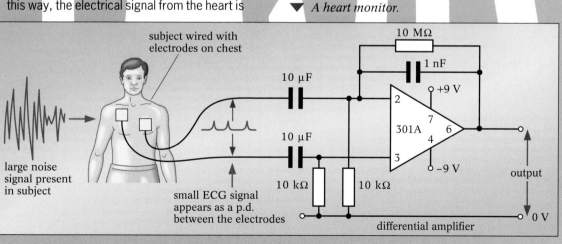

Electronics for people with visual impairment

The Braille alphabet was one of the very first systems designed to help people who are visually impaired. It was invented by Louis Braille who lived from 1809 to 1852 and was blind from the age of three. His alphabet uses a system of raised dots to represent letters. It enabled blind people to read and is still widely used today. For example, computers with Braille keyboards are available.

▼ *An example of Standard English Braille.*

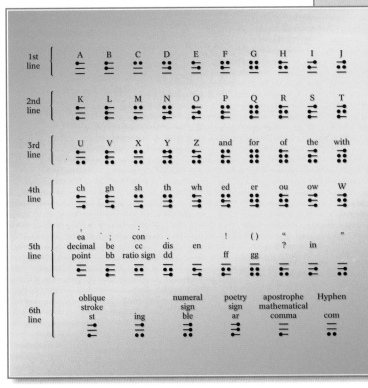

There are about 1 million people in the UK who are registered as blind or partially sighted, and this number is growing every year.

This activity will help you to realise the problems with which visually impaired people have to cope. It may also give you ideas for 'design-and-make' activities.

You need to work with a trusted friend. One of you should wear a blindfold. Try moving around the school and carrying out some everyday activities. Your 'sighted' friend should stay with you all of the time. Get your friend to keep a record of the problems you encounter.

Many visually impaired people choose to carry a white stick. This helps other people to know that their sight is impaired but it is also used to help them move around. It can be swept in front of them to check that the path is clear. Specially trained guide dogs are also used.

What are the advantages and disadvantages of white sticks and guide dogs?

▲ *Person getting about with a stick.*

Crossing the road

This system uses *infrared* transmitters mounted at street corners; you carry the receiver. The system gives you signals, telling you when you are approaching a road, when you have reached the other side, and so on. It may be possible to use such a system to give you information about where you are, what facilities are nearby, bus-stops, local shops, and so on.

Investigating infrared

Many *optical devices* use infrared (IR) rather than visible light. There are several advantages to using infrared. For example, infrared devices are easily shielded from other light, and infrared is invisible.

◀ *Person crossing the road using an infrared transmitter/receiver system.*

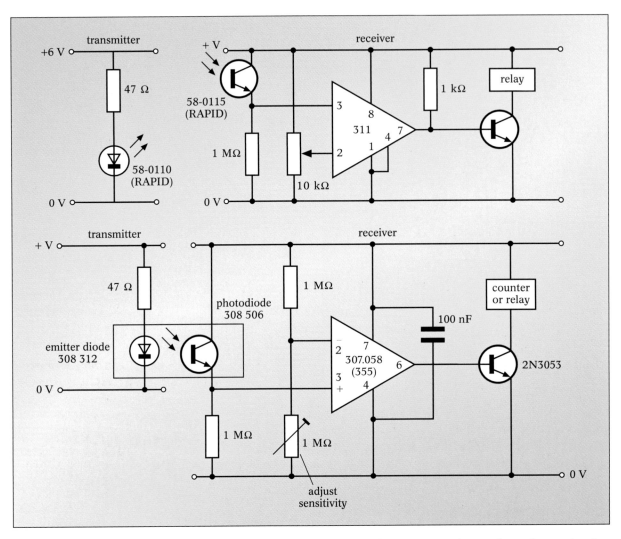

▲ *An infrared transmitter and a receiver – two alternative circuits. The relay is energised when it receives a signal from the transmitter and can be used to control a suitable indicator.*

Use one of the circuits given to make an infrared transmitter and a receiver.

Use the transmitter and receiver combination to investigate:
- the distance the signal travels,
- what happens when you reflect the signal through different angles,
- whether the signal travels through different materials, and how far the signal travels through different thicknesses of materials.

The circuit on page 67 is another alternative for the transmitter and receiver combination. The transmitter is based on a 555 timer circuit in its 'astable' mode. Each time the switch is closed, the transistor switches the LED on and off at a frequency of 5 kHz.

More about ... the 555 timer pages 102–103.

The pulse of infrared from the transmitter falls on the photodiode of the receiver. The signals are amplified and passed to the *filter*, where any background signals or noise are cut out so that only the 5 kHz signal passes through to the final amplifier stage.

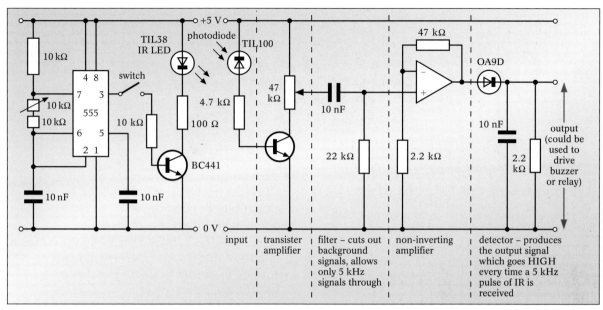

▲ *A third infrared transmitter and receiver circuit diagram.*

The detector produces the output signal, which goes 'on' every time a 5 kHz pulse is received. This output signal can be used to drive a buzzer, and used, latched, to drive a relay or other output device.

You should now know about:
- **some of the ways in which electronic devices may assist visually impaired people,**
- **infrared transmission and reception.**

You should now be able to complete one of the tasks below, which may form part or all of your coursework.

More than half of the visually impaired people living in the UK live alone. Make a list of all the problems they are likely to encounter. Here are some ideas to help you.
- Taking the correct amount of medicine.
- What is the difference between a can of hair spray and a can of oven cleaner?
- How do you know when it is time to bring in the washing because it is raining?
- What is the difference between a £10 and a £20 note?
- Controls on cookers and other household equipment.
- Pouring boiling water – how do you know when the cup is full?
- Cutting a loaf of bread.

How could electronics help in these situations? Is an electronic solution the simplest and cheapest option? Use the information you have to design and make a device to help people with a visual impairment.

In the future, all electrical devices in the home could be connected to a central processor or computer. How could this help people who are visually impaired?
Develop a simple computer control package that activates a number of devices using an infrared beam.

More about ... product development pages 76–79.

More about ... making electronic products pages 82–86.

Other sources of information

Royal National Institute for the Blind (RNIB)
World Blind Union, 58 Avenue Bosquet, 75007 Paris, France

Contexts for control

Electronic or computer control systems are used in many areas of everyday life because:

- they enable quick and accurate control of the processes used in industry, business and leisure, which are often very complicated and have to work very quickly,
- they can help to maintain the quality of a product and to reduce waste,
- they enable processes to keep running all the time,
- they assist us in running many processes concurrently (at the same time) or consecutively (one after the other),

- the conditions in a process are often more efficiently monitored and adjusted by electronics or computers,
- failure warnings (for parts used in a production process) are easily incorporated into the control system, so reducing the amount of production time lost due to maintenance and repair,
- they can be used as part of safety and security systems.

▼ *Control systems are essential in a chemical plant.*

In this chapter, we shall look at six very different contexts (situations) where control systems are used, which should give you ideas for 'design-and-make' activities. The contexts we shall look at are:

- a bottling plant,
- environmental control in a commercial glasshouse,
- a supermarket,
- an automated warehouse,
- a Channel Tunnel train – *Le Shuttle*,
- a theatre.

You could analyse one or more of the contexts and see where and how control systems are used, or use these examples as starting points to help you to analyse a context of your own. This context may come from any relevant source or opportunity. For example, you could be inspired by:

- an industrial or other visit,
- a need for control systems in your school or at home,
- your hobbies or interests,
- suggestions from your teacher.

> **More about ...** analysing a control system pages 80–81.

Remember that your control system may be electronic, computer-based or a mixture of the two. You must decide which type of control system is best.

Remember also that your system must operate safely. If anything goes wrong the system should shut down to a **fail-safe** position, where no harm can come to anyone operating the system or working within the environment.

 A bottling plant

The bottles are moved along conveyor belts or around turntables towards a filling point, where they are filled automatically with the correct amount of liquid. The bottles are then moved on to be capped and packaged. A control system must monitor and regulate all these processes.

> Why is it important to fill the bottles as quickly as possible?
> Give reasons why the amount of liquid put into each bottle must be carefully controlled.

Analysing the system
Here, we will concentrate on the part of the system that controls the moving and filling of the bottles. The following questions will help you to analyse the system.

- How are the empty bottles moved to the filling point?
- How is each bottle stopped in the correct position?

A bottling plant. ▶

- How can the system tell if a bottle is empty, and not already filled?
- How are the bottles filled?
- How is each bottle filled to the correct level?
- How can the system tell when the bottle is filled to the correct level?
- How long must each bottle stay in the filling position?
- How are the bottles moved on?
- What happens if one of the steps in the process stops working correctly?

Select one of the following design briefs for the bottling plant. Design and model a control system to the brief. First, produce a flow-block diagram of the system and then analyse this in more detail. This analysis should enable you to develop a detailed specification for the system.

Brief 1
It is important to move the bottles to the correct position and then stop them for a set time.

Brief 2
The bottles must be filled to the correct level. When the bottle is in position the filling device should start. When the bottle is full it should stop.

A commercial glasshouse

Glasshouses provide conditions that ensure plants grow quickly and successfully. These conditions must be controlled carefully to produce exactly the correct environment for the plants. The conditions, such as temperature, light, humidity, and so on, must therefore be monitored constantly and altered if necessary. The best way to do this is by using an automatic control system. The following questions will help you to analyse the system.

- Is the growing medium (usually soil) at the correct temperature?
- Is there frost protection?
- Are the plants getting enough light?
- Could artificial light be used to extend the growing period?
- Is the moisture level in the medium correct?
- Is the humidity of the air correct?
- Is the acidity of the soil correct for the plants being grown?
- Is the proportion of carbon dioxide in the atmosphere correct?
- Is there too little (or too much) ventilation?

The ideal conditions will be different for different types of plants.

More about ...
analysing control systems pages 80–81.

Heating system in a ▶ commercial glasshouse.

What do you think are the three most important conditions to monitor and control?

You could analyse each of your three selected areas separately. For each one, you would need to:

- explain why monitoring and controlling the condition is important,
- identify the type of control sub-system that is most suitable,
- identify where the condition should be monitored (for example, the temperature should be monitored in the air inside and outside the glasshouse, possibly at several positions, and at several places in the growing medium),
- draw a flow-block diagram for the sub-system you have chosen,
- list the input and output sensors and transducers that you could use.

Select one of the following design briefs for the glasshouse. Design and model a control system to the brief. First, produce a flow-block diagram of the system and then analyse this in more detail. This analysis should enable you to develop a detailed specification for the system.

1 Night-time frosts occur quite often in early spring. These frosts can damage plants in the early stages of their growth. The glasshouse needs a device that will either warn the glasshouse staff of a possible frost or switch on a heater. It is likely that the frosts will occur during the night, so the staff would prefer the second option!

2 During the early stages of growth, plants require considerable amounts of moisture in the growing medium, to ensure that they grow quickly and without disease. If the medium becomes too dry, the plants will wither and may die. If the medium is too wet, the roots will rot. A control system is needed to keep the moisture levels suitable for the plants. Remember that some plants are grown hydroponically – their roots are submerged in a liquid stream of nutrients that flows continuously, rather than being buried in soil. The system should be capable of controlling both soil-based and hydroponic environments.

3 The humidity (moisture content) of the air in the glasshouse should be kept at a fairly constant level, to ensure good plant growth. Output devices that affect humidity include water sprays and devices that alter ventilation. The temperature also has an effect on humidity – more water will evaporate from the growing medium in a warm glasshouse than in a cold one. This evaporation will increase the air humidity, but reduce the moisture content of the growing medium.

If there is sufficient time, you could produce a complete working model of an automated glasshouse. You could also consider scaling up one or more of your systems and testing them in a full-size domestic glasshouse.

More about ... analysing control systems pages 80–81.

A supermarket

Here are three areas where control systems are used in supermarkets:

- regulating the conditions in areas where food is stored,
- controlling the use of energy to improve energy efficiency,
- monitoring the quantities of products bought and sold, so that stock levels can be maintained.

Make a list of other areas in a supermarket where control systems are used.

Energy management

Modern supermarkets require large amounts of energy for lighting, heating and air conditioning, running refrigerators and freezers, operating in-store bakeries, and so on. Control systems ensure that energy is used as efficiently as possible. Large stores built today use only 60% of the energy of a new store built ten years ago, despite the fact that new stores today are on average three times bigger than they were ten years ago!

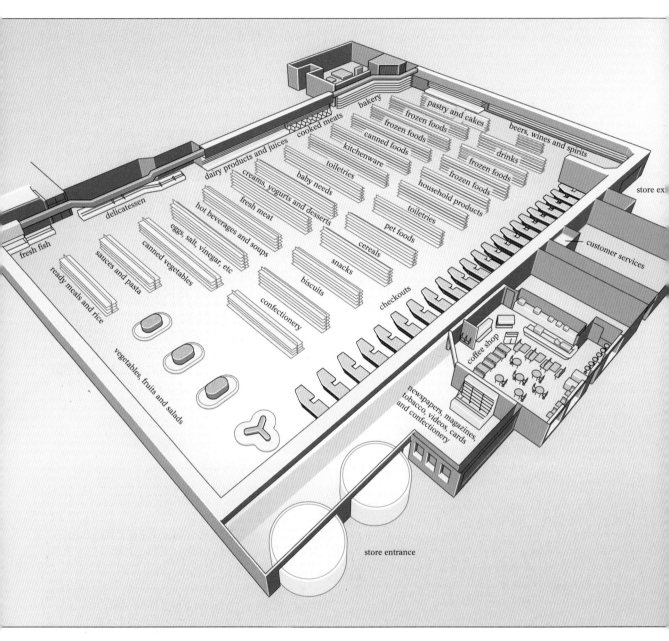

▲ *Plan of a supermarket.*

One important way of reducing energy consumption is to make use of waste heat from refrigerators, freezers, lights and the ovens in the bakery. The recycled heat can be used for, say, heating the storage area or warming air in the air-conditioning system.

A computer-based system is the most effective way to monitor, control and report on the energy used for heating, ventilation, air-conditioning and lighting.

Analysing the system

Here are a number of systems that you could investigate:

- controlling temperature in freezers and refrigerators,
- monitoring the waste heat from freezers, refrigerators and lights,
- monitoring the temperature in the store to control the heating system,
- controlling the light levels in the store.

Select one of these systems for the supermarket. Design and model a control system. First, produce a flow-block diagram of the system and then analyse this in more detail. This analysis should enable you to develop a detailed specification for the system.

If you work in a group, you may be able to cover many of the areas outlined above. You could then produce a complete working model of an energy management system.

More about ... analysing control systems pages 80–81.

More about ... computer control pages 30–43.

An automated warehouse

In a large warehouse containing a wide variety of items, many people may be needed to find and collect those items. Parts of this process could be automated. A typical system might use a vehicle that follows a series of lines on the floor. Different patterns of lines guide it to different areas of the warehouse. When the vehicle arrives at the correct location, a collecting device moves vertically to find the correct level in a stack and then horizontally to take an item from the stack. An alternative is a partially automated system, where an operator sits on the vehicle. The vehicle moves to the correct place and the operator takes the required item from a storage bin.

This system can be controlled using a computer. The computer can process the orders, control the vehicle to retrieve the items, and keep a record of how much stock has been used. It can also order new stock when necessary.

▼ *Inside a large warehouse.*

More about ... computer control page 30.

Select one aspect of the control of the warehouse, then design and model a control system to carry out that function. First, produce a flow-block diagram of the system and then analyse this in more detail. This analysis should enable you to develop a detailed specification for the system.

You could make a model of the retrieval vehicle using a construction kit such as Fischertechnik or LEGO. You could control your vehicle using a computer.

If you work in a group you may be able to cover many of the areas outlined above. You could then produce a complete working model of the warehouse management system.

More about ... analysing control systems pages 80–81.

Le Shuttle

The Channel Tunnel connects France and England. In fact, there are really three Channel tunnels, connected to each other at points along their length. There are two railway tunnels and a service tunnel. There are complex control systems to maintain safety and security. Three types of train use the Channel Tunnel – *Eurostar* passenger trains, freight trains and *Le Shuttle* trains. *Le Shuttle* carries vehicles and their passengers from England to France (or from France to England) in less than 30 minutes. You can turn up at the terminal (there is no need to book in advance), pay your fare, pass through passport and ticket controls, and drive onto a train.

Control systems are used on the trains to maintain safety, comfort and security for passengers and staff. In the passenger–vehicle wagons, the temperature is maintained between 18 and 22 °C, and there is a temperature display for passengers to see. The air humidity is also controlled. When vehicles are loaded and unloaded, carbon monoxide levels are monitored. There are also sensors that detect the presence of flammable gases such as propane and butane, which come from sources such as leaking camping cookers.

Analysing the system

Select one of the conditions to monitor and control, and analyse the situation in detail. You will need to:

- find out the range within which the condition must be maintained, and the levels at which to operate an alarm,
- identify an input sensor to detect the condition,

▲ *Le Shuttle.*

- decide what output transducers are required,
- decide whether a display or alarm is needed,
- decide whether the display or alarm should be audio, visual or both,
- consider the needs of all of the users of the system.

The system must also have a **fail-safe**. For example, if the system breaks down due to a power failure, an alarm should sound automatically or there should be some other clear warning that the system is malfunctioning.

Select one aspect of control in the Channel Tunnel, then design and model a control system to carry out that function. First, produce a flow-block diagram of the system, and then analyse this in more detail. This analysis should enable you to develop a detailed specification for the system.

You could also investigate the use of computer control in the area you have considered.

More about ... computer control pages 30–43.

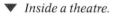

▼ *Inside a theatre.*

A theatre

Control systems are used in many ways in a modern theatre. For example, the lights are dimmed or brightened, positioned and focused to fit in with the action on the stage. Control systems can also be used to lower or raise pieces of scenery, and to operate special effects such as trapdoors, smoke and explosions. In some theatres, revolving platforms are used for scene changes. The stage curtains are often operated using a remote control system.

Make a list of as many areas as you can where control systems could be used in a theatre. Inspect your school stage or arrange a visit to a local theatre. Decide what systems you will investigate further.

Select one aspect of control in the theatre, then design and model a control system to carry out that function. First, produce a flow-block diagram of the system, and then analyse this in more detail. This analysis should enable you to develop a detailed specification for the system.

You could also investigate the use of computer control in the area you have considered.

More about ... analysing control systems pages 80–81.

More about ... computer control pages 30–43.

More about ... control in the theatre *What a performance!* STEP 5–16 Key stage 3 Context book.

Product development

The success of any product in a competitive market depends on careful product development. This process may involve designing, testing and producing an entirely new product. The development of products can also involve incorporating new components, materials or manufacturing methods into an existing product. For example, the development of a washing machine could involve updating the electronic controls. Other developments involve the use of major new inventions or advances in technology. For example, improvements in desktop computers often involve the development of new processing chips.

Look at the products in the photograph. List those that are the result of new inventions, and those that are improvements of previous designs using updated technology.

▼ *Everyday electronic products.*

Milestones

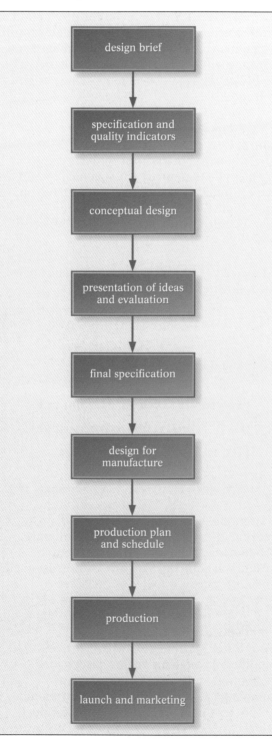

▼ *A milestone plan.*

A *milestone plan* breaks up a development process into a sequence of stages (milestones). Each milestone must be completed successfully before you can move on to tackle the next milestone.

We shall now look at each milestone in product development. This should help you to structure your thoughts and time as you progress through your own projects, whether you are using electronic or computer control.

Design brief

A *design brief* is a statement of the broad objectives and requirements of a product that is to be developed. The minimum requirement for a design brief is a statement of the product's basic function – what it must do.

A design brief may include more than this. For instance:

- evidence of actual or potential customer demand,
- indication of target user group,
- basic performance requirements,
- target costs and selling price,
- special features of the product,
- advantages over existing and/or competing products,
- guidelines on appearance, style and image,
- list of legal requirements, standards and codes of practice,
- requirements for reliability and durability,
- recommended materials, components and quality of finish,
- use of standard components,
- *ergonomic* requirements,
- safety requirements,
- timetable and deadlines for production.

Many of these points will be developed in the detailed specification, and need only be broad guidelines at this stage.

Specification and conceptual design

A *specification* turns the design brief from a set of general objectives into a more detailed list of technical, manufacturing and market requirements. The production of a detailed design specification is one of the most important steps in successful product development. Producing the specification may involve further market research and technical *feasibility studies*. A feasibility study will usually provide answers to the following questions.

```
Can it be done?

Can it be done in time?

Can it be done within
the budget?
```

The specification should also set down *quality indicators*, used to check both the quality of the design and the quality of the final product.

Successful product development matches the product to the needs of the market. As you develop your specification, you need to talk to the potential users of your product. You will use your specification both to evaluate your product as you work through your project, and to judge the effectiveness of your final product. You may need to alter your specification as you encounter problems during development.

Conceptual design involves developing several alternative designs. Sketches, drawings, mock-ups and models are produced to test their basic feasibility. In the design of electronics and control systems, this involves the production of models using systems kits and computer control programs, trying ideas out on breadboard and working with models. It is important to sort out at this stage as many problems in the design as you can.

Evaluation

The evaluation of the conceptual designs enables you to improve the specification. At this stage, production issues become much more important. Quality indicators for the manufacturing process should be developed now.

At the very least, the evaluation should answer the following questions.

```
Is the product marketable?

Does it meet the quality
standard?

Does it use standard
pre-manufactured components?

Will it meet the target price?

Can it be made within the
target cost?
```

You should continually refer to your specification to ensure that the developing product meets the requirements. Your evaluation could also involve external agencies and customers.

Final specification

Your initial specification will have been modified through modelling, discussion, evaluation and so on. When you have completed all of these activities, you should produce a final specification of the product, which will be carried through to manufacture.

Design for manufacture

Design for manufacture means producing a product that meets the specification and quality required, can be produced at or below the target cost, and can be sold at the target price. Good system design means using as few components as possible and being as economical as possible with other resources. This keeps costs down and makes manufacturing easier. Trade-offs between production and customer requirements may have to be made. But, in designing for the market, production considerations should not dominate the design process.

Production plan and schedule

A *production plan* should detail:

- the sequence of actions involved in the manufacturing process,
- when and where raw materials are needed in the process,
- when and where equipment is needed,
- when and where production staff are needed,
- the types of assembly process required,
- the quality checks required.

A *production schedule* lists target dates or times for key stages in the manufacturing process. In this way, you can keep track of the production and make alterations to the plan as necessary.

Launch and marketing

You will need to think carefully about how you will market your product, for example what type of advertising you will use and the shops that will sell it. You will need to think about how the product will be packaged and what effect this may have on costs.

Analysing and developing control systems

This chapter gives guidance on how to tackle projects requiring control. The process described here can be applied to any situation where control systems are required. After reading this chapter, you should have a better idea of what you should be doing when you come to analyse your own control problem. The prompts are intended to form a framework around which you can build your own ideas. Some may not be appropriate for your project; others may just put you on the right road.

You should carry out a thorough analysis of your control 'problem' before you decide on your control system. The first step is to break the problem down into simpler stages and ask yourself questions about the requirements of the system.

When you have answered the questions, produce a flow-block diagram to show each stage of the problem. Look at each of the blocks in your diagram in turn, and draw a flow chart to show what the block does in detail. Your flow chart should show:

- any decisions that have to be made,
- the stages at which a control system could be used,
- what the control system would do.

Now analyse your flow chart to decide which control system would be best for the job.

- What type of control system could you use for each part of the flow chart?
- Will your system use **open-** or **closed-loop control**?
- What input sensors and output transducers will you use?

Identify the conditions that should be controlled and the sequence of operations that have to be performed.

> **More about …** control systems page 108.

> **More about …** system terms page 6.

> **More about …** sensors and transducers pages 92–101.

Design your system using flow-block diagrams, showing how the various parts are connected. Each of these blocks can be treated later as a separate sub-system.

Decide what type of control is needed for each sub-system:

- open-loop control (no feedback),
- closed-loop (feedback) control, which can be either simple on/off control or continuously variable control,

- control using logic gates,
- computer control.

> **More about ...** open- and closed-loop control pages 12, 108.

> **More about ...** logic gates page 107.

> **More about ...** computer control pages 30–43.

In each case you may need to:

- identify the sub-systems required,
- investigate and test the input sensors needed,
- investigate and test the output transducers needed,
- investigate signal processing and matching between sub-systems.

When matching the sub-systems in your control system, you will need to consider not only the electronic signals, but also any links where electronic signals are converted to mechanical actions (and vice versa). Analyse the input, process and output stages of each sub-system. Draw a flow-block diagram to show the components of each sub-system.

Make sure that the output from one sub-system matches the input requirements of the next sub-system. In particular, you will usually need a power driver for an output transducer. The output may require a separate power supply controlled by a relay or a high-power driver.

> **More about ...** powering output devices pages 97–98.

You should ask yourself the following questions.

- Does your power supply have the capacity to provide the voltage and current required by the whole system and any output devices ?
- Can you provide the correct voltages for each part of the system?
- Does the output of each stage in the system provide the current needed as the input for the next stage?
- Does each output driver match its output device?

When you have a complete system in flow-block diagram or flow chart form, use whatever materials are best to model your system and investigate whether it will work. You could use:

- paper,
- card,
- plastic sheets,
- thin sheet metal (for simple shapes),
- other resistant materials,
- construction kits,
- pneumatics kits,
- electronic systems kits,
- computer control programs and interfaces.

> **More about ...** basic electronics pages 90–101.

> **More about ...** integrated circuits pages 102–107.

Making and testing electronic products

The easiest way to try out design ideas and make a prototype is to use an electronic systems kit. You can try a range of ideas very quickly and be sure that stages in the design are compatible (the output signals from one sub-system match the input requirements of the next sub-system). Some electronics kits include extra boards, sometimes called prototype boards, so that you can make separate sub-systems. If you do not have a systems kit, you can use a breadboard to construct a prototype circuit.

Build and test your prototype one stage at a time – this makes it much easier to test the circuit and change components. Build and test sub-systems separately if possible.

Producing a circuit diagram and PCB mask

There are a number of computer programs available that enable you to produce photographic acetate masks for your design. These masks can be used to make a printed circuit board (PCB). Some programs can also be used to plot your designs directly on to the PCB. A library of artwork files, to assist you in designing your system on computer, is also available for

systems kits from Quality Learning Services, Kingston Centre, Fairway, Stafford, ST16 3TW.

A number of drawing packages are available that can be used to create your own systems artwork. Two examples are Corel Draw! and Autosketch.

Making a PCB

The diagram opposite summarises the method of making a PCB from an acetate mask. Use a magnifier to check your PCB for bridges and gaps.

- Bridges are where the copper is left between tracks when it is not needed. You can remove these with a craft knife.
- Gaps are breaks in the copper track where it should be continuous. You can solder a piece of wire across these gaps.

Program	Computer	Supplier
Quick Track	BBC	NCET
FastTrax	Archimedes	Techsoft
Quickroute3.5	PC	Power ware/Economatics
McCAD	Macintosh	Capedia
Easy PC	PC, Macintosh	Number One Systems Ltd

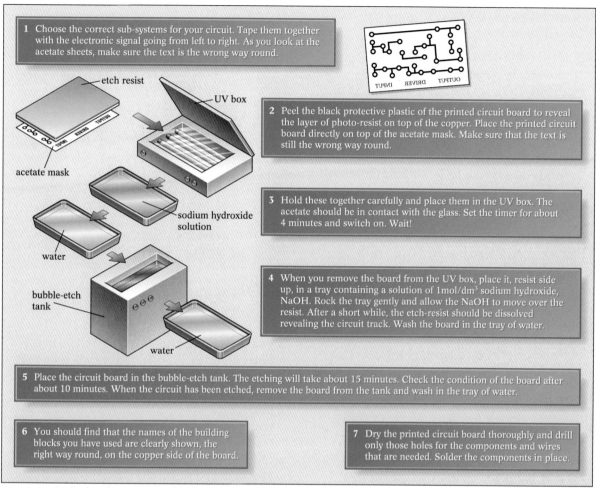

1 Choose the correct sub-systems for your circuit. Tape them together with the electronic signal going from left to right. As you look at the acetate sheets, make sure the text is the wrong way round.

etch resist

UV box

acetate mask

2 Peel the black protective plastic of the printed circuit board to reveal the layer of photo-resist on top of the copper. Place the printed circuit board directly on top of the acetate mask. Make sure that the text is still the wrong way round.

sodium hydroxide solution

3 Hold these together carefully and place them in the UV box. The acetate should be in contact with the glass. Set the timer for about 4 minutes and switch on. Wait!

water

bubble-etch tank

4 When you remove the board from the UV box, place it, resist side up, in a tray containing a solution of 1mol/dm³ sodium hydroxide, NaOH. Rock the tray gently and allow the NaOH to move over the resist. After a short while, the etch-resist should be dissolved revealing the circuit track. Wash the board in the tray of water.

water

5 Place the circuit board in the bubble-etch tank. The etching will take about 15 minutes. Check the condition of the board after about 10 minutes. When the circuit has been etched, remove the board from the tank and wash in the tray of water.

6 You should find that the names of the building blocks you have used are clearly shown, the right way round, on the copper side of the board.

7 Dry the printed circuit board thoroughly and drill only those holes for the components and wires that are needed. Solder the components in place.

▲ *A method of making a PCB from an acetate mask.*

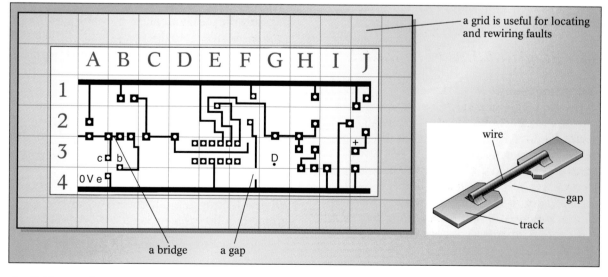

a grid is useful for locating and rewiring faults

wire

gap

track

a bridge   a gap

▲ *Bridges and gaps.*

Assembling a circuit

Follow these rules.

- Build one sub-system at a time.
- Start with the power supply and work methodically, from the input stage of the first sub-system through to the output stage of the last sub-system.
- Test each sub-system once it is complete.
- Only move on to the next sub-system when the one you are making is working correctly.

Mounting components

There are two ways of mounting components on the circuit board. Traditionally, holes for the components are drilled through the PCB, the components are inserted and the connections are soldered in place. However, there has been a move throughout industry towards **surface mounting** components directly on to the copper tracks laid down on the PCB. This technique requires special heat resistant glues as well as solder.

Drilling holes

Use a 1.0 mm bit fitted to a high-speed drill to produce the holes you need to mount components.

Some components (such as preset potentiometers) may require a larger diameter hole, hence you will need a larger drill-bit. You will also need a larger drill-bit if you need mounting holes, to place the circuit inside a container.

Surface mounting

If you surface mount components, you do not have to drill any holes in the PCB for the components. You must ensure that the copper tracks have been produced the correct way around. When you get to part 1 of the 'Using the acetates' process (page 83), *do not* reverse the acetate mask. When you have made your PCB, the tracking on it should be the same way round as the circuit diagram it represents.

Soldering

When soldering components onto a drilled board, follow this process.

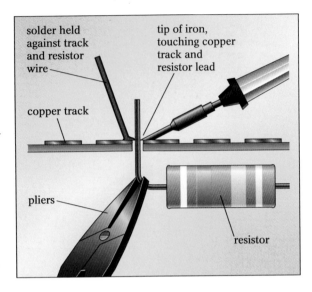

▲ *Soldering components onto a PCB.*

- Insert the components through the correct holes in the PCB, so that they stick out on the track side of the PCB.
- Hold the component by the leg with small pliers. This will help to dissipate the heat of the soldering iron and avoid damage to the component.
- Use a soldering iron with a clean, hot tip. Hold the tip against the copper track and the leg of the component.
- After a few seconds, hold the solder wire against the joint and allow a small amount of solder to melt onto the track.
- Remove the solder, then the soldering iron.
- Do not allow any movement of the joint while the solder is cooling.
- Pull gently on the component to make sure that it is fixed securely. Use a multimeter to check for electrical conductivity.
- Cut the surplus length of lead off using a side-cutter.

When soldering components to be surface mounted, follow this process.

- Decide how close to the PCB you want to solder the component.
- Cut off any surplus length of leads on the component with a side-cutter.

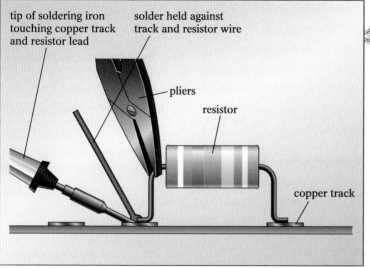

▲ *Soldering components onto a PCB – surface mount.*

In the diagram labels:
- tip of soldering iron touching copper track and resistor lead
- solder held against track and resistor wire
- pliers
- resistor
- copper track

- Hold the component by the leg with small pliers and place it on the track.
- Now follow the instructions for soldering as described above.
- You may find you need someone else to help hold things when surface mounting components.

Selecting the correct power supply

Follow these guidelines when selecting a power supply for your device. The power supply must:

- provide the voltage required,
- be capable of supplying the current required.

A battery must match the use of the device, for example continuous use with low current drawn over a long period of time or high current taken in short bursts.

You can find details of suitable power supplies in electronics catalogues.

Fault-finding

Some techniques for fault-finding within electronic systems are described in this section. Fault-finding is a skill that improves with experience. People develop a feel for where problems usually lie and how they can be solved. However, there are some techniques you can learn that will cope with a wide range of problems with electronics.

You will probably have access to two types of measuring instrument:

- a multimeter used either as an ammeter to measure current flow or as a voltmeter to measure voltage,
- an oscilloscope to give a 'picture' of what is happening to the signal in different parts of the system.

More about ... multimeters page 88.

More about ... oscilloscopes page 88.

When using an electronic systems kit you will begin to appreciate:

- the types of signals that some electronic building-blocks produce,
- the types of signals that some electronic building-blocks need to make them work,
- the way in which some signals are altered by electronic building-blocks.

You can then transfer your knowledge of the basic operation of the building-blocks to your circuit. You should know what to expect from the different parts of the circuit.

Be systematic when fault-finding in a system. A system should be designed and constructed so that you can work through it logically – building-block by building-block. This is true both when the system is in kit form and when it has been made up as a printed circuit. You should:

- always keep a careful record of what you do,
- develop some kind of tick list or chart of problems for which you will test.

Here is a good method for working through your systems tests.

1 Be clear what each section of the system is intended to do before you carry out any testing or fault-finding.
2 Check that the power supply has been switched on and that the power supply is connected the right way round (the *polarity* is correct).
3 Check that each part of the system has power (use a voltmeter to test this).
4 Work through the system stage by stage from the input to the output, making sure that the signals at each stage are what you expect.
5 If you suspect a faulty building-block, replace it with an equivalent block that you know works.
6 Do not replace individual components in a building-block one by one – this can introduce even more faults. If you find that a system fault appears to come from a particular building-block, remove it from the system and test it on its own with known input signals.
7 Use circuit diagrams of the building-blocks to help you if the fault persists.

When working with printed circuit boards, some of the ideas listed above will be useful. You should also consider the following points.

1 Inspect the circuit for:
  - broken tracks,
  - missing components,
  - components incorrectly placed,
  - wrong values of components,
  - faulty solder joints,
  - broken wires,
  - blown fuses.

You will need your circuit diagram to check these points.

2 Check the artwork you have used to make the circuit board with the circuit diagram.

3 Measure the voltage where the signal is transferred from one sub-system to another. For example:
  - on the base of transistors,
  - on the collector of transistors,
  - on power lines to microchips,
  - on inputs to and outputs from microchips.

4 Work out the voltage or current values that you expect at each point then check that each voltage or current value is what you expect, and work logically and consistently from the input to the output. (You could repeat this by working backwards from output to input as a check.)

5 Only when you have narrowed down the fault to a small area should you start to replace components (carefully). Retest the circuit each time you replace a component.

The suggestions here are in no way exhaustive. Add any techniques that you find useful and you know will work. The key to fault-finding is to be systematic.

> **More about ...** fault-finding see sheets 88–90 in *STEP Key stage 3 Datafile*.

 *Testing circuits*

You should test the operation of your circuit as you build each stage. You will have fewer things to test as you go along and it should mean that the complete circuit is more likely to work first time. Some rules for testing are listed here.

Testing a cell or battery

You should check the voltage across a battery both:

- on *open circuit* – with no current being drawn from the battery, and
- with the circuit switched on – when current is being drawn.

The battery may seem to be working correctly when no current is being drawn, but the battery may not be able to provide the current needed by the circuit.

Testing a component out of the circuit

Test the electrical *resistance* of the component.

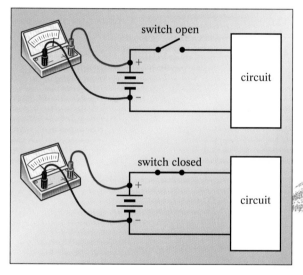

switch open

circuit

switch closed

circuit

▲ *Measuring the voltage across a battery.*

Testing a component in the circuit

Make sure that the circuit is switched off when you make a resistance measurement. One end of the component should be disconnected from the circuit. This is to ensure that you measure only the resistance of the component and not the resistance of the rest of the circuit. You must also disconnect one end of a component in this way if you measure *capacitance*.

Testing the operation of a stage in the circuit

Tests that you are likely to perform include:

- measuring voltages using a multimeter,
- investigating a signal using an oscilloscope,
- checking the state of a stage in the circuit using a logic probe.

The circuit must be switched on for all of these tests. The test instrument must be set to the correct range. The COMMON (COM) terminal of the instrument should be connected to the negative or 0 V line of the circuit. Connect the positive terminal of the instrument to the point in the circuit you want to investigate.

Instruments for testing

There are three main instruments used to test electronic circuits. These are listed in the table below.

More about ... logic states page 107.

Instrument	Uses	Features	Notes
multimeter	measuring resistance, voltage and current	can be set to different ranges can be analogue or digital can measure a.c. and d.c. signals	must be set to the correct range for the quantity you wish to measure
cathode-ray oscilloscope (CRO)	investigating input and output signals investigating wave forms	can measure a.c. and d.c. signals, time and frequency	setting up a CRO can be quite complicated
logic probe	checking the logic state of a circuit (high/on or low/off)		

Multimeters

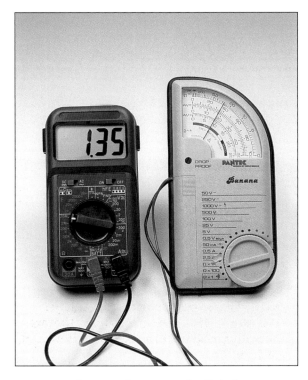

▲ *An analogue multimeter and a digital multimeter.*

Analogue multimeters enable you to observe constant or slowly changing signals. They can be used to measure voltage, current and resistance. However, they are more difficult to use than digital meters (especially when measuring resistance). They also have a comparatively low internal resistance, and can therefore affect the voltage you are trying to measure. This can be a particular problem if you are measuring the voltage across a high resistance value.

Digital multimeters can also be used to measure constant signals, but are not very effective at displaying changing values. They are easier to read than analogue meters, and will also measure voltage, current and resistance.

Digital multimeters have a comparatively high internal resistance, and therefore have little effect on a voltage being measured.

Cathode-ray oscilloscope (CRO)

Oscilloscopes can be single- or dual-beam. A dual-beam oscilloscope allows you to look at two signals at the same time.

Connections to the oscilloscope are usually made using a length of coaxial cable, which may have a crocodile clip and a probe to attach to components or circuit stages. The basic controls on an oscilloscope are as follows.

● The *timebase* sets the sweep rate – the speed at which the signal is swept across the screen. You can use this to produce either a slow-moving spot across the screen or a continuous trace. The time divisions will be in ms or µs (thousandths or millionths of a second) per screen division.
● The *voltage gain*, which allows you to set the voltage range being measured or to take approximate measurements of voltage from the oscilloscope screen. The voltage divisions will be in mV per screen division.

You should look carefully at the oscilloscope(s) you have in your school and familiarise yourself with the controls.

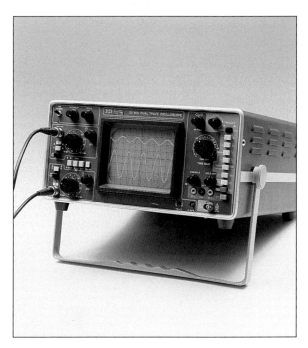

▲ *A dual-beam oscilloscope.*

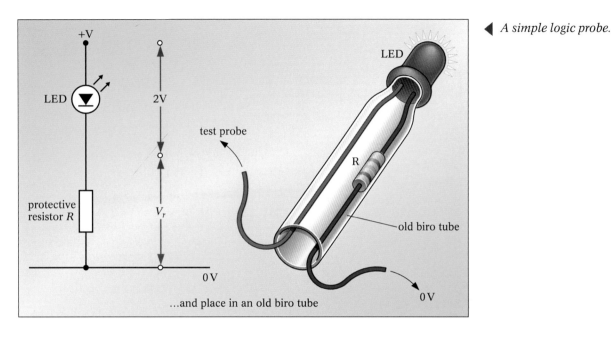

A simple logic probe.

LED

test probe

LED

R

old biro tube

0 V

...and place in an old biro tube

Logic probe

You can test the logic state of any point in a circuit using a logic probe, which in its most simple form consists of an LED with a protective resistor.

A single LED requires a voltage of about 2 V across it to work. The current through an LED varies from about 5 mA to 20 mA. To avoid damage to the LED, a protective or limiting resistor must be used. The value of this resistor depends on the supply voltage used. For example, for the probe in the diagram the value can be calculated as follows.

If the supply voltage is V, then the potential difference across the protective resistance V_r will be:

$$V_r = V - 2$$

Suppose the maximum current through the LED is 10 mA. This current also flows through the limiting resistor. The value of the resistor, R, is given by:

$$R = \frac{V_r}{I}$$

$$R = \frac{V - 2}{I}$$

A supply voltage of 9 V gives a value for R of 700 Ω. The nearest available resistor value is 680 Ω. (Manufacturers make resistors in a range of convenient values; you have to use a 'nearest available' value if the particular resistor you need is not available. You can also make particular resistances by combining smaller resistors.)

More about ... potential difference page 90.

Basic electronics

Current and potential difference

An electric current is the flow of electric charge through a conductor. The flow of electric current is measured in amperes. The notation for amperes is 'A' and the symbol for electric current is 'I'. In electronic systems, you will measure currents as small as a few millionths of an ampere (microamperes, µA) or thousandths of an ampere (milliamperes, mA).

Potential difference or p.d. is a measure of the voltage between two points. It is measured in volts. It is possible for a potential difference to exist between two points without an electric current flowing. The notation for volts is 'V' and the symbol for p.d. or voltage is 'V'. You will measure p.d.s as small as a few millivolts (mV).

A battery of cells or a power supply is used to provide a source of current. By convention, electric current is said to flow from the positive terminal of a power supply, through the circuit to the negative terminal of the power supply.

There are two types of power supply system: direct current (d.c.) and alternating current (a.c.). The voltage of a d.c. supply does not change with time. The voltage of an a.c. supply varies *sinusoidally* with time, from a maximum in one direction, through zero to the same maximum in the other direction, and back again. Most of your electronic systems will require only low voltage d.c. power supplies.

Resistance

A *load* offers opposition (**resistance**) to electric current. Resistance is measured in ohms. The notation for ohms is 'Ω' and the symbol for resistance is 'R'. You may come across resistances of several thousand ohms (kilohms, kΩ).

▼ *Current, potential difference and resistance in a circuit.*

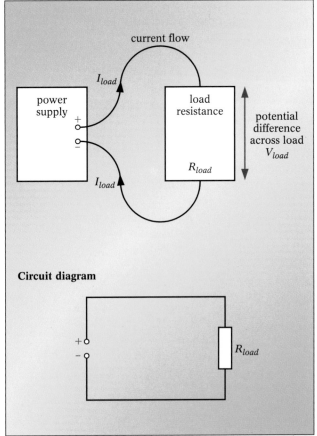

For the circuit shown, if V_{load} is measured in volts and I_{load} is measured in amperes, the resistance in ohms of the load device, R_{load}, is given by:

$$R_{load} = \frac{V_{load}}{I_{load}}$$

For a metal conductor, this resistance is constant for any voltage or current so long as its temperature stays constant. If the conductor heats up (as it may well do if a high current flows), the resistance will change.

Series and parallel connections

The diagram below shows how total resistances are calculated in series and parallel circuits.

▼ *Series and parallel connections.*

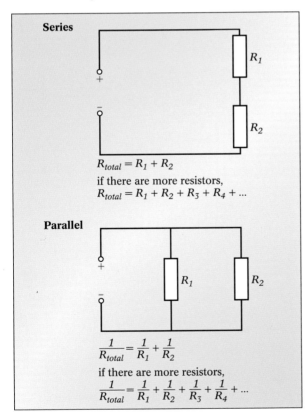

The potential divider

A **potential divider** consists of two (or more) resistors connected to a power supply so that output voltages can be taken from across each of the resistors.

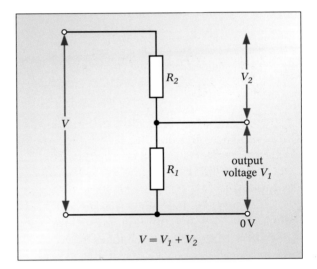

▲ *Potential divider.*

This is called a potential divider because it divides up a potential difference. The potential divider is an important sub-system in electronics and control work. It can be used in several ways.

- *To provide a fixed reference voltage.*
  If the resistors R_1 and R_2 in the diagram are both fixed then a set voltage V_1 will be produced at the output.

- *To provide an adjustable reference voltage.*
  If either the resistor R_1 or R_2 in the diagram is replaced with a variable resistor, then a variable voltage V_1 will be produced at the output.

- *To provide an input voltage using a sensor.*
  Many types of sensor can be connected into a potential divider to convert changes in physical conditions (like temperature) into changes in voltage. Either of the fixed resistors in a potential divider circuit can be replaced by a sensor.

Sensors in potential divider-type circuits

Most of the circuits that follow are based on the potential divider sub-system, but some are alternative sub-systems that perform the same function as a potential divider.

> Build the following circuits on prototype board, or investigate them using your electronic systems kit, before you use them in an electronic or computer control project. In this way, you should gain a better understanding of how the sub-systems work.

Thermistors

The resistance of a thermistor changes with temperature, although the change in resistance is not *linear* (the resistance changes by a different amount for each 1 °C change in temperature). The thermistors commonly used in temperature-sensing circuits have a negative temperature coefficient. This means that the resistance of the thermistor decreases as the temperature increases. The output voltage therefore changes with temperature. Sometimes a variable resistor is needed in the circuit to ensure that the output stays within a reasonable voltage range.

Diodes

A diode can be used with an op-amp to provide a linear change in resistance with temperature. With the values shown in the diagram, the output voltage will fall by about 40 mV when you hold the diode between your fingers.

▼ *Using a diode to detect temperature changes.*

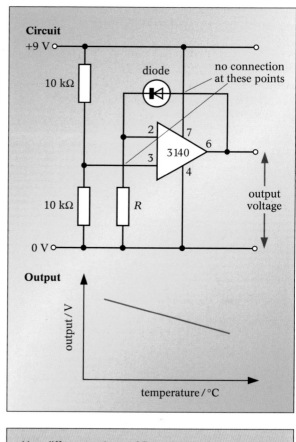

> Use different values of *R* to give the temperature range you need.

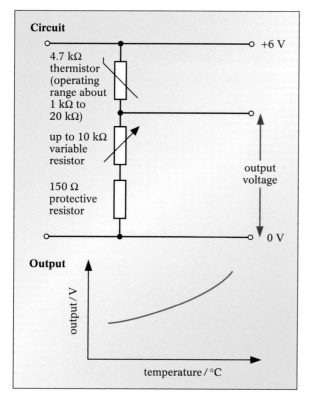

▲ *A thermistor in a potential divider.*

Thermocouples

A thermocouple consists of one wire made from one metal, and another wire made from a different metal, joined together at one end. If the temperature of the junction changes, then there is a change in potential difference between the other ends of the wires. Thermocouples give a linear output and can work over a very wide temperature range.

The thermocouple circuit shown here will provide a 1 V change in voltage for a 100 °C change in temperature. It therefore has a sensitivity of 10 mV per °C.

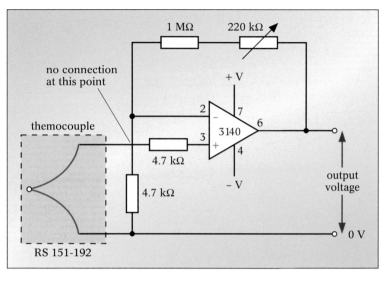

▲ *A thermocouple circuit.*

LM35 integrated circuits

The LM35 is a purpose-made temperature sensor chip. It provides a linear output with a sensitivity of 10 mV per °C. Two versions are available, one covering the temperature range 0 °C to 100 °C and one covering –40 °C to +110 °C. The LM35 can be used as a temperature probe.

Light-dependent resistors

The resistance of a light-dependent resistor (LDR) changes with the level of light falling on it. The most commonly used LDR is the ORP12. This has a working range of 1 kΩ in bright light to 100 kΩ or more in the dark. You may need to use a variable resistor in place of R_1 to obtain a particular range of output voltage. The output from an ORP12 is not linear.

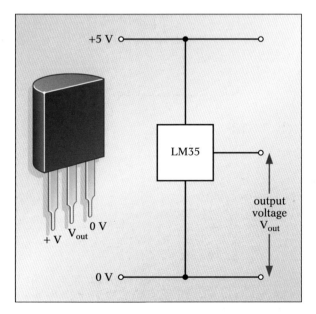

▲ *The LM35 integrated circuit.*

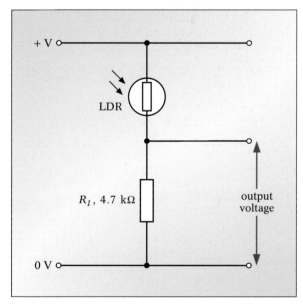

▲ *An LDR in a potential divider.*

Photodiodes

A photodiode can be used with an op-amp to provide a linear output that is dependent on the light falling on it.

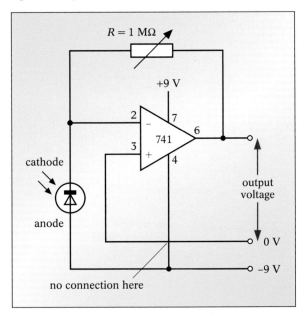

▲ *Using a photodiode to provide a linear output.*

Phototransistors

A phototransistor can be thought of as a photodiode and a transistor combined. The phototransistor produces and amplifies a signal in response to changing light levels.

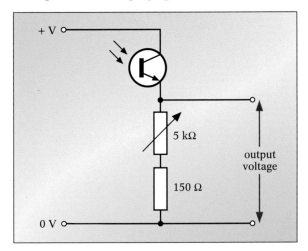

▲ *A phototransistor.*

The table contains a summary of light sensors.

Sensor	Advantages	Disadvantages
LDR	cheap simple circuit needed large change in resistance	slow response non-linear large in size
photodiode	fast response linear relatively small	complex circuit needed
phototransistor	can drive small loads directly faster response than an LDR	non-linear

Moisture sensors

This is the simplest type of moisture sensor. It can be made from two copper strips or rods, or etched from a piece of printed circuit board. It is not very sensitive and is likely to give only an on/off response.

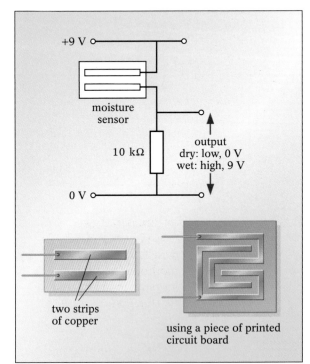

▲ *A moisture sensor.*

Humidity sensors

A humidity sensor can be used to monitor moisture levels in the air. The output voltage will vary from about 24 mV to about 1500 mV as the relative humidity changes from 20% to 80%. The output is not linear. The output voltages are shown in the table.

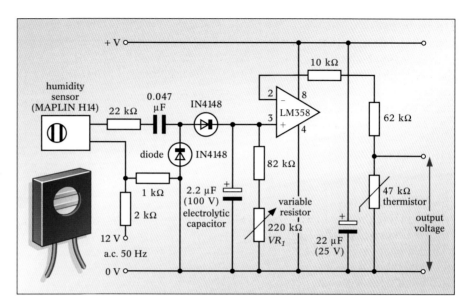

▲ *A commercial humidity sensor and the circuit needed.*

Output voltage/mV	Relative humidity/%
24.3	20
66.5	25
156	30
303	35
545	40
807	45
1052	50
1235	55
1354	60
1429	65
1471	70
1498	75
1519	80

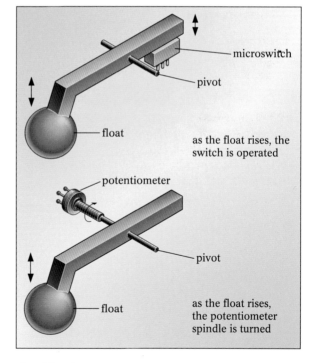

▲ *A level sensor.*

Potentiometers and microswitches

A liquid level can be sensed mechanically, by using a lever-operated switch or a potentiometer. Both methods use a float as the level detector. The microswitch provides a digital (on/off) signal and the potentiometer provides an analogue signal.

Microswitches can be used in a number of other ways. They are useful as limit switches, which can be used to stop a motor in a particular position, or as position switches, which detect when something is at (or passing) a particular point. Microswitches can be connected into a potential divider sub-system.

Optoswitches

Optoswitches make use of an infrared beam. If the beam from a slotted optoswitch is broken (or the beam from a reflective optoswitch is reflected), the circuit output signal changes.

You can make a wheel or strip with holes that rotates inside the slot of a slotted optoswitch. The infrared beam is only detected when it passes through a hole. You can use this to count numbers of revolutions or measure speeds of rotation.

The reflective optoswitch can be used as a barcode reader or line follower.

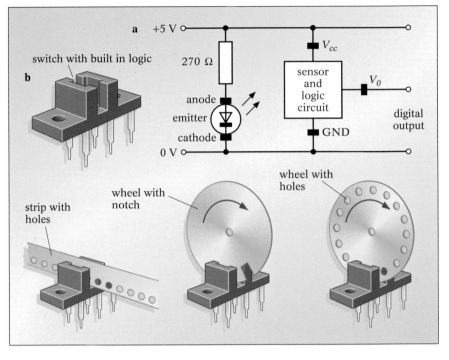

▲ *A slotted optoswitch:* **a** *the circuit;* **b** *using the switch as a counter.*

To select an input sensor you need to consider:
- the range for which it can be used,
- its sensitivity,
- whether you need a linear output,
- its response time,
- its cost,
- its availability,
- where it can be used (for example, can it be used in a liquid?),
- the complexity of the signal processing needed.

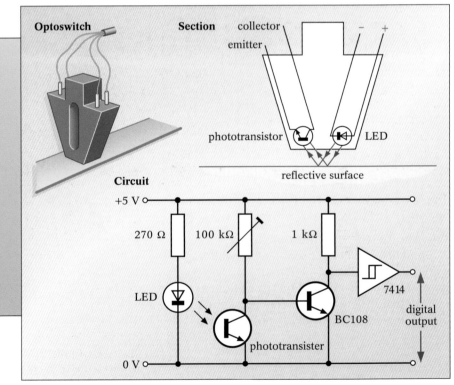

▲ *A reflective optoswitch.*

Powering output devices

There is a wide range of transducers that can be used as output devices. Transducers convert one form of energy into another. In electronic systems, these transducers usually convert electrical energy into a physical response. Lamps, buzzers, relays, solenoids and pneumatic cylinders are all transducers.

In an electronic system, each stage or sub-system must provide enough current to drive the next stage or sub-system. However, output devices all have different current requirements, and the signals produced by an electronic system may not be suitable to drive an output device directly. However, the signal can be used as the input to a *transducer driver*, which can provide the current required to drive the output device.

There is a wide range of transducer drivers available. Some of them are summarised in the table, together with typical applications.

The basic action of a transistor is as a switch. Bipolar and MOSFET transistors are different in construction and input requirements to standard transistors, but behave in very much the same way when used as transducer drivers.

- If the input voltage is low, the transistor behaves like an open switch and the output device is off.

Transducer driver	Typical maximum current/A	Output devices driven
Transistor, e.g. BC108	0.1	LEDs buzzer some relays
ZTX300	0.5	small motors relays
BFY51	1.0	bulbs
Darlington pair TIP110	2.5	solenoids larger motors larger relays
Power transistors 2N3055	3.0	any of the above and other high current devices
TIP33	10.0	
MOSFET MPT3055A	12.0	

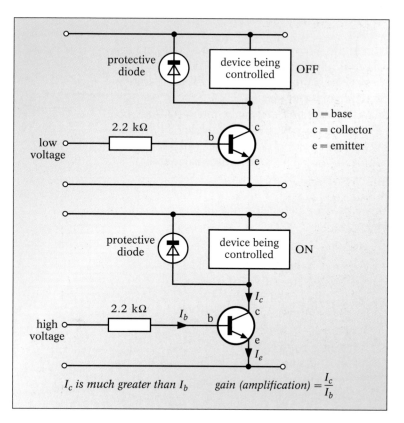

I_c is much greater than I_b

$$\text{gain (amplification)} = \frac{I_c}{I_b}$$

▲ *The operation of a transducer driver.*

- If the input voltage is high, the transistor behaves like a closed switch and the output device is on.

The collector current I_c is much larger than the base current I_b. The small base current switches on the larger collector current.

Various other devices may be used as transducer drivers, for example CMOS devices, solid-state relays, thyristors, triacs, mechanical relays and so on. With all of these examples, you will need to match the power requirements of the output device with the characteristics of the driver.

There are many different textbooks available that deal in detail with power matching and current flow in output devices.

Output devices

Relays

For simple on/off control systems you can use a **relay**, which is an electromagnetic switch that uses a small current through a coil to operate a switch in another circuit. This second circuit has a separate power supply, meaning that you can use it to power an output device if it needs a supply voltage greater than the control circuit supply voltage. The relay must be capable of taking the current needed by the load.

You can arrange the contacts in a relay in one of two ways.

- Normally open (NO) – the device being controlled is normally off. The circuit containing the device is switched on by energising the relay.
- Normally closed (NC) – the device being controlled is normally on. The circuit is switched off by energising the relay.

There are several types of relays; some are capable of switching more than one circuit at a time. You may come across SPDT (single pole, double throw) and DPDT (double pole, double throw) relays. These terms refer to the number of contacts and ways of switching that a relay possesses.

▼ *Modes of switching.*

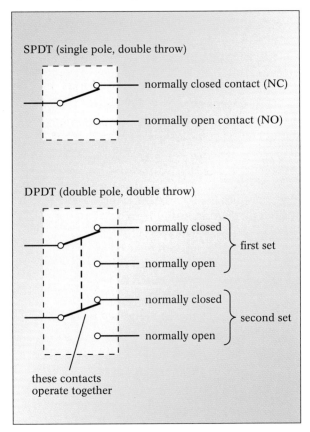

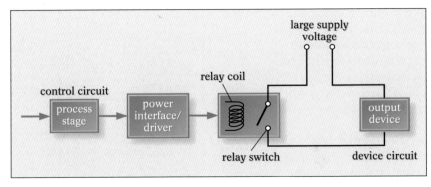

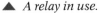
▲ *A relay in use.*

Motors

Motors can be used for positional control, and their speed can be controlled if continuous movement is required. Microswitches can be used to switch a motor on or off in set positions. The motor output can be reversed using double pole changeover switches or a DPDT relay.

Motors generally turn at high speeds. A gearbox will slow down (or speed up) the output if this is required. If a gearbox is used to slow down the output, this increases the torque (turning force) supplied by the output. The speed of the motor is usually most easily controlled by altering the voltage supplied. One problem with this method is that the torque drops as the motor speed is reduced. The diagram shows a better motor speed controller, which uses a power transistor. The speed is controlled by switching the transistor on and off rapidly at different rates.

Motors can also be used as input sensors. If the motor is forced to turn, it acts as an electrical generator. The current produced by the generator depends on how fast it is turned. You can measure the speed of rotation by measuring the output current.

Servo motors

Servo motors operate at slow speeds, but produce high torque (turning forces). They can be turned to a set position very accurately. If the motor is forced out of position, internal feedback detects this and the motor will try to return to the set position. This makes them useful for operating valves.

Servo motors can be operated by a pulsed signal. The duration of the signal controls the amount of movement. This signal is provided by a servo motor driver.

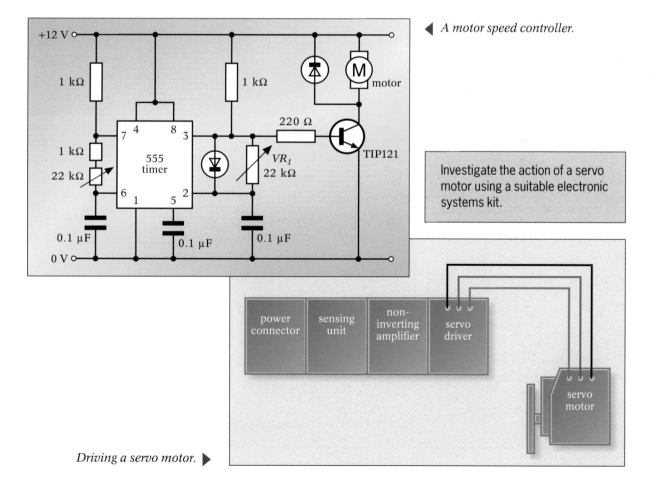

◀ *A motor speed controller.*

Investigate the action of a servo motor using a suitable electronic systems kit.

Driving a servo motor. ▶

The servo motor driver requires an analogue input voltage. You can use any sensor as the input (a light sensor works well). A non-inverting amplifier is used to process the output signal from the sensor.

> **More about ...** light sensors pages 93–94.

Stepper motors

Stepper motors are used to provide very accurate control of movement. The motor moves around in a series of steps; typically each step is a turn through 7.5 degrees. The stepper motor therefore makes 48 steps in one full revolution (360 degrees). Stepper motors that make 1.8 degree steps (200 steps to one revolution) are also available. Stepper motors do not have high torque, and are most suitable for driving light loads requiring precise control. However, once the motor is in position, if the power supply is maintained, the motor locks, and a large force is needed to make it move. Stepper motors are controlled by special drivers, one example of which is the SAA1027.

You need to provide a series of pulses at the STEP input. You can produce these pulses using a 555 timer IC or a computer interface. The motor is reversed by changing the logic state at pin 3 (hence DIR for direction).

> **More about ...** 555 timers pages 102–103.

> **More about ...** logic states page 107.

Solenoids

A solenoid is an electromagnet, which can operate a plunger or a lever.

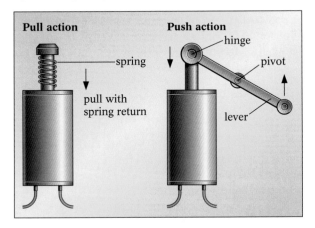

▲ *Types of solenoid.*

▼ *A stepper motor drive circuit.*

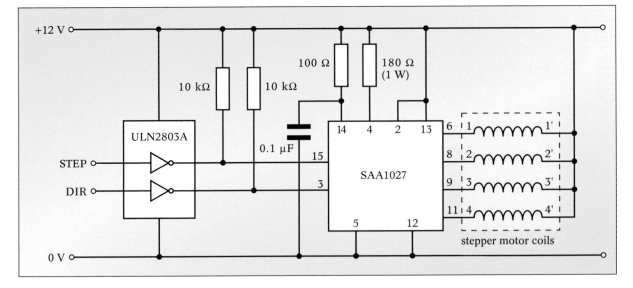

There is a range of solenoids that operate on 12 or 24 volt direct current. For example, RS Components RS347-652 (push action) and RS349-709 (pull action). Some features of solenoids are listed below.

- They use relatively large electric currents.
- They must be controlled using a power driver (the electric current has to flow all of the time the solenoid is switched on, which can lead to overheating and means they have a large power consumption).
- They only work in one direction – the plunger moves either out or in when the solenoid is activated – and the return to the original position often requires a spring.
- They operate very quickly.
- They are best used to provide a large force over a small distance. Levers can be used to amplify the distance moved, but this will reduce the applied force.

Two valves operated by solenoids are shown below. They are used to control the flow of liquids, and can be controlled using on/off or proportional control systems. *Proportional control* means that the amount the valve is open can be varied to control the flow (like a tap).

> **More about ...** types of control pages 108–109.

You can make your own solenoid or servo motor-operated valve using a piece of flexible tubing. The solenoid can be used directly or with a lever. Servo motors have a range of attachments that could be used.

Pumps

Pumps are used to control the flow of liquids and gases. A pump is easy to switch on and off, but is difficult to use with proportional control. A suitable pump for liquids that you could use is a car windscreen washer pump, which operates at 12 V.

> You may find that a car windscreen washer pump produces too fast a flow of liquid for your needs. Investigate running the pump at reduced voltage to achieve your desired rate of flow.

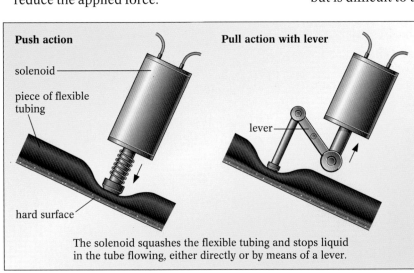

Push action

solenoid

piece of flexible tubing

hard surface

Pull action with lever

lever

The solenoid squashes the flexible tubing and stops liquid in the tube flowing, either directly or by means of a lever.

▲ *Controlling a simple valve with a solenoid or a servo motor.*

Integrated circuits

This chapter provides information about some useful integrated circuits (ICs). The circuits covered are:

- the 555 timer used either as an astable or as a monostable,
- the operational amplifier (op-amp) used in a variety of ways,
- logic gates and their truth tables.

The 555 timer IC

This can be used as a pulse generator, and can be set up either as a **monostable** or as an **astable**. A monostable system has only one stable state – it can be made to change but it will always return to the same stable state. An astable system has no stable state – it changes continually from one state to the other.

The monostable timer
In this circuit, the output device (an LED, a buzzer or a relay) will be turned on for a set time. The length of the pulse can be altered by changing the resistor R_1 and/or the capacitor C_1. You can calculate the approximate time of the pulse (t, in seconds) using the formula

$$t = R_1 \times C_1$$

▼ *A 555 set up as a monostable.*

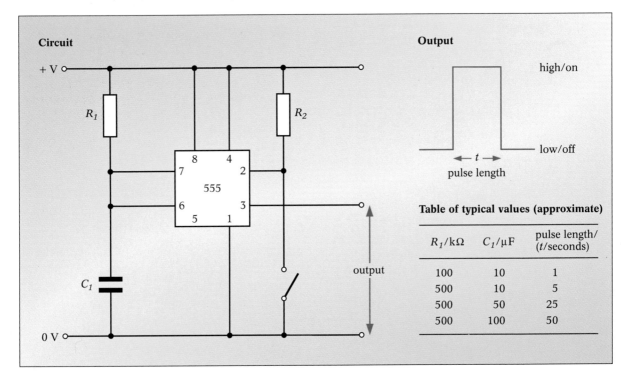

R_1/kΩ	C_1/μF	pulse length/ (t/seconds)
100	10	1
500	10	5
500	50	25
500	100	50

Table of typical values (approximate)

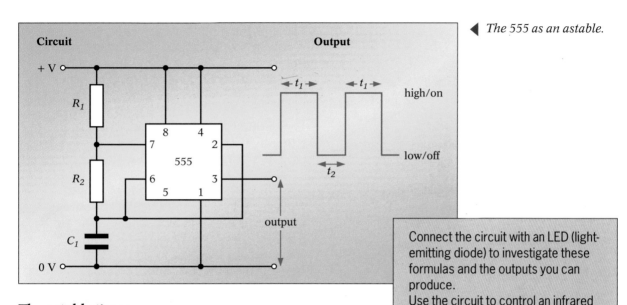

The 555 as an astable.

The astable timer

A 555 timer IC can be arranged as an astable – both the on and off pulse length can be controlled by the external components.

The approximate high or on time is given by the formula

$$t_1 = 0.7 \ (R_1 + R_2)C_1$$

The approximate low or off time is given by the formula

$$t_2 = 0.7 \ R_2C_1$$

The *frequency* of the pulses can be calculated using the formula

$$f = \frac{1.44}{C_1(R_1 + 2R_2)}$$

If R_2 is made very much larger than R_1 then the on and off times become equal. The frequency in this case is given by

$$f = \frac{0.7}{C_1 R_2}$$

Connect the circuit with an LED (light-emitting diode) to investigate these formulas and the outputs you can produce.
Use the circuit to control an infrared transmitter.

More about ... infrared transmitters pages 66–67.

The operational amplifier

There are several IC op-amps available, including the 741, the TL081 and the 3140. All are 8-pin packages. An op-amp requires positive, zero and negative voltage connections, which means that a special power supply or two separate supplies (such as two cells) have to be used. The applied voltage can be between 5 V and 14 V. The 741 is cheaper but the output voltage will not go below 2 V. This is not low enough to turn off a transistor.

Op-amps can be used in circuits in many ways, to perform the following functions:

- comparator,
- differential amplifier,
- inverting amplifier,
- non-inverting amplifier,
- constant-current generator,
- Schmitt trigger,
- square-wave oscillator.

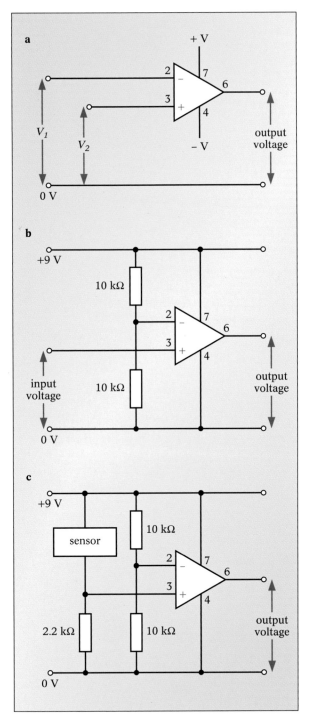

▲ *Three comparator circuits.*

The comparator

A comparator compares a set voltage level with the actual level. The output voltage from the comparator depends on the relative values of the two input voltages.

The output voltage will be digital (it can be either high or low), so the comparator can be used as a simple analogue-to-digital converter.

In **a**, the op-amp compares the two input voltages. If V_1 is greater than V_2, the output is negative. If V_2 is greater than V_1 the output is positive. If $V_1 = V_2$, the output is nominally zero.

In **b**, the op-amp compares the voltages applied at pins 2 and 3. Pin 2 is at 4.5 V because the two resistors act as a potential divider, dividing the 9 V supply into two equal parts.
If the input voltage is higher than 4.5 V, the output is high.
If the input voltage is lower than 4.5 V, the output is low (close to 0 V).

In **c**, if the resistance of the sensor is less than 2.2 kΩ, then the voltage at pin 3 is more than 4.5 V and the output is high.
If the resistance of the sensor is more than 2.2 kΩ, the voltage at pin 3 is less than 4.5 V and the output is low.

The easiest way to investigate a comparator is to use an electronic systems kit.

You will need:
- a power supply and power connector,
- an input voltage unit,
- a comparator,
- two voltmeters or multimeters.

Connect the circuit boards as shown in the diagram. Notice that the comparator has two inputs (labelled A and B) and only one output (labelled C). Connect one voltmeter (V$_2$) to measure the output voltage. The other voltmeter (V$_1$) will be used to measure the voltages at different points on the circuit. Connect the negative terminal to the negative rail and a flying lead to the positive terminal.

You can use the input voltage unit to change the voltage at point A, and the potentiometer on the comparator to change the voltage at point B. Use voltmeter V$_1$ to measure the voltage at A and at B.

What happens to the output voltage at point C when:
- the voltage at A is higher than the voltage at B,
- the voltage at B is higher than the voltage at A?

Use the voltmeter V$_1$ to compare the signals at A and B.

▲ *Circuit board connections for a comparator.*

The differential amplifier
- If the voltage at pin 2 is greater than the voltage at pin 3, the output is negative.
- If the voltage at pin 3 is greater than the voltage at pin 2, the output is positive.
- If the voltage at pin 2 equals the voltage at pin 3, the output is nominally 0.

The difference between the two input voltages can be very small, but will affect the output because the op-amp amplifies the difference between the two input signals. The gain of the op-amp in this configuration is very large, so even small differences between the inputs cause very large differences in output.

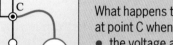

▼ *Differential amplifier.*

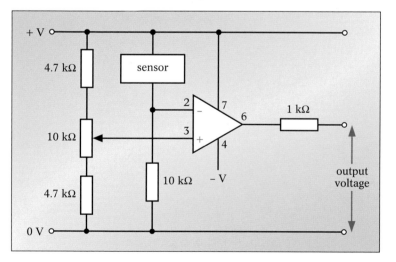

The inverting amplifier

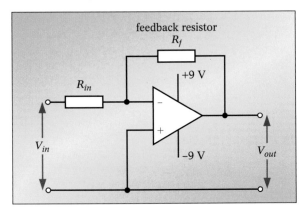

▲ *Inverting amplifier.*

The input signal is applied to pin 2, the inverting input. If a positive input voltage is applied to the input resistor, R_{in}, the output will go negative. If a negative voltage is applied to the input resistor R_{in}, the output will go positive. The voltage amplification or gain is given by:

$$\text{gain} = \frac{V_{out}}{V_{in}} = -\frac{R_f}{R_{in}}$$

The non-inverting amplifier

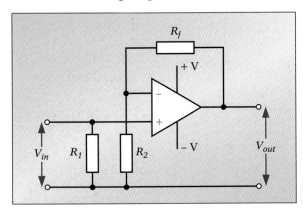

▲ *Non-inverting amplifier.*

The input signal is applied to pin 3, the non-inverting input. When V_{in} goes positive, V_{out} goes more positive. The gain is given by:

$$\text{gain} = \frac{V_{out}}{V_{in}} = \frac{R_f + R_2}{R_2}$$

The constant-current generator

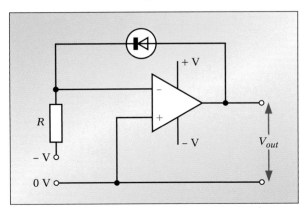

▲ *Constant-current generator.*

More about ... constant-current generator page 56.

The Schmitt trigger

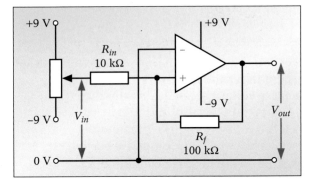

▲ *Schmitt trigger.*

A Schmitt trigger is an electronic circuit that can be used to convert analogue signals into digital signals, or to 'clean up' noisy signals.

More about ... Schmitt triggers page 58.

$V_s = $ switching voltage

$$= \frac{R_{in}}{R_f} V_{out}$$

The square-wave oscillator

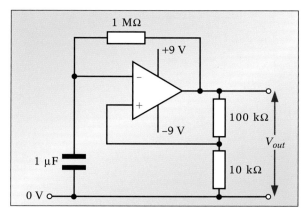

▲ *Square-wave oscillator.*

A square-wave oscillator is a circuit that produces regular pulses. It may also be called an astable multivibrator.

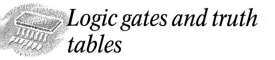 *Logic gates and truth tables*

▼ *The symbols and truth tables for commonly used logic gates.*

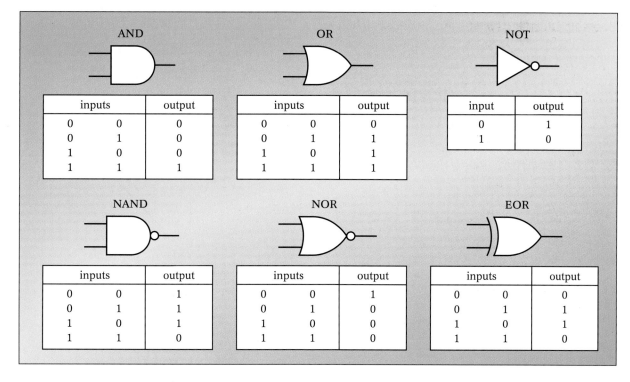

Control systems

Try out some of these activities as you meet them in your project work. Use prototype board or parts of your electronic systems kit to model the ideas before using them in your projects.

There are two main types of continuous control system:

- open-loop control, which does not use feedback,
- closed-loop control, which does use feedback.

Open-loop control

With open-loop control, once a system is operating it will continue without hindrance from the controlled system. No feedback signal is used to inform the input stage what is happening at the output.

More about ... open-loop control pages 12, 26–29.

Closed-loop control

In closed-loop control systems, information is fed back and combined with the input signal to modify the output signal.

Feedback control can be either *on/off* (sometimes known as *two-step*), where the feedback signal is either on or off, or *proportional*, where the feedback signal can have a range of values.

More about ... feedback pages 12–13.

On/off or two-step control
The feedback signal is used to switch the controlled heating element fully on or fully off. Examples of its use include temperature control in rooms or buildings and water heating systems.

More about ... temperature control pages 26–29.

▼ *Open-loop motor control. If the motor is loaded, its speed will decrease and it may stall – no steps are taken to correct this.*

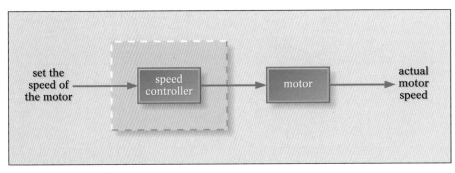

On/off heating control. ▶

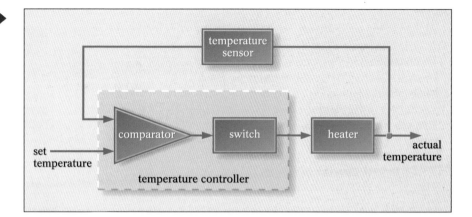

Proportional control

In this example, a sensor attached to the motor detects changes in speed and sends a signal back to the speed controller. The controller adjusts the speed of the motor accordingly.

This is an example of negative feedback. Any difference between the set speed of the motor and its actual speed produces an error signal. The size of the error signal depends on how far the actual speed is from the set speed. Negative feedback systems work to reduce the size of the error signal to zero and stabilise any changes in the outputs.

▲ *Proportional motor speed control.*

More about ... error signals page 13.

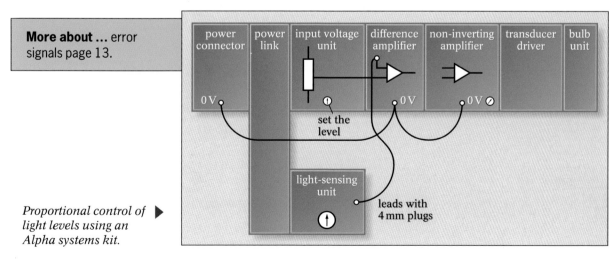

Proportional control of ▶ *light levels using an Alpha systems kit.*

Construct the light-sensing circuit shown on page109 using an electronic systems kit. Set the potentiometer on the light-sensing unit to the mid-position. Set the gain on the amplifier to about 3. Adjust the potentiometer on the input voltage unit so that the lamp is just off. Cover the light sensor with your hand and then move your hand away slowly to increase the amount of light falling on the sensor. See if you can get the level of illumination to remain constant.

Sequential control

Systems often use *sequential control*. This means that actions take place one after the other. Each action depends on the previous one having been carried out. For example, the wash cycle in an automatic washing machine might be:

1 fill with water,

2 heat water,

3 wash,

4 pump out water,

5 stop.

The sensors in various parts of the washing machine send signals to the controller to ensure that actions have been carried out. This is an example of where a computer control program would be better than a hard-wired electronic circuit.

More about ... computer control pages 30–43.

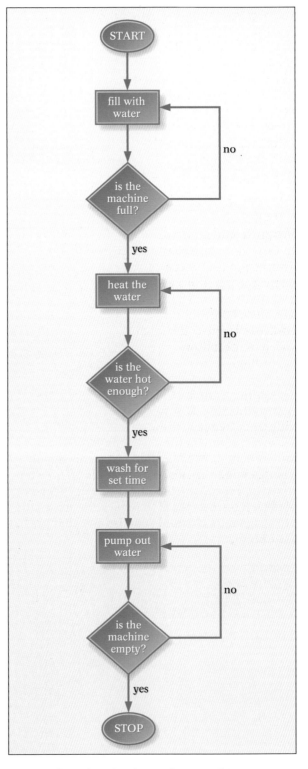

▲ *The flow chart for the washing machine sequence.*

Controlling systems using logic

The water heating sub-system in the washing machine is a good example where logic can be used. For safety reasons, the water heater should only switch on when:

- the door is closed, and
- the water level is high enough, and
- the water is cold.

This heating action can be triggered by a logic circuit.

The truth table for the combinational logic circuit would be as follows:

More about ... logic gates page 107.

▼ *A diagram of the water heating sub-system.*

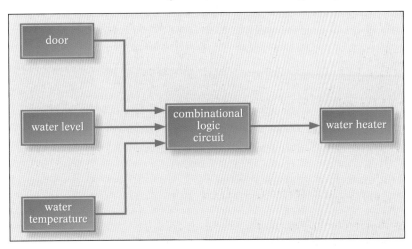

	Inputs			Output
	Door	**Water level**	**Water temperature**	
	0	0	0	0
	1	0	0	0
	0	1	0	0
	0	0	1	0
	0	1	1	0
	1	0	1	0
	1	1	0	1
	1	1	1	0
	0 = open 1 = closed	0 = low 1 = high	0 = cold 1 = hot	0 = off 1 = on

Glossary

Analogue signal
A signal that can take any value between limits.

Analogue-to-digital conversion
Converting analogue signals into digital signals.

Astable
An electronic sub-system that produces a stream of pulses. It can be triggered or allowed to run continuously.

Binary signal
A digital signal with only two values – high (on) or low (off). (*See also* digital signal.)

Boundary
The limits within which a system is being investigated.

Closed-loop control
This is when the output of a system has an effect on the input to the system, which in turn can cause a change in the output.

Comparator
A sub-system that compares two electronic signals and produces an output signal that depends upon their relative strengths.

Digital signal
A signal that can take only certain values between two limits. (*See also* binary signal.)

Digital-to-analogue conversion
Converting digital signals into analogue signals.

Error signal
The difference in signal strength between an input signal and the feedback signal.

Fail-safe
If anything goes wrong with an electronic system, a fail-safe switches the system to a state that will cause no harm to anyone. A fail-safe may also switch on a back-up system to provide any vitally important functions.

Feedback
A signal that is sent from the output of a system to the input of that system, to modify the way the system behaves.

Flow chart
A diagrammatic way of representing events, effects and decisions.

Hard-wired system
An electronic system.

Hunting
The inability of a system to settle down into a stable state.

Hysteresis
The difference between the voltage at which a device will switch on and the voltage at which it will switch off. *See* Schmitt trigger.

Input
A signal which is sent into a system.

Interfaces
Devices which allow electrical signals into and out of a microcomputer.

Lag
The time delay between causing a change and the change having any effect.

Monostable
An electronic sub-system which produces a single pulse when triggered and then switches off.

Noise
Unwanted electrical signals.

Open-loop control
This is when the output of the system has no effect on the subsequent input to the system.

Operational amplifier (op-amp)
A very versatile electronic sub-system which can be used to provide a range of functions from amplifying to pulse generating.

Optical fibre
A thin, flexible glass or plastic rod, usually coated with a layer of plastic, through which light signals travel.

Oscillate
To move continuously between two limits (can be digital or analogue).

Output
The effect of a system in the physical world.

Potential difference
The difference in voltage between two points in an electrical circuit.

Potential divider
A very important sub-system which is used to split (divide) the voltage up into a number of parts. The potential divider is used as the basis of many electronic sensors.

Procedure
A group of commands which carries out a particular function (a control program sub-system).

Process
An action or operation which causes a change in the signal as it moves through a system.

Relay
An electrical switch.

Resistance
The opposition to the flow of current by electronic components.

Schmitt trigger
An electronic sub-system which has two different switching levels – an upper switching level when it switches on and a lower switching level when it switches off. The difference between these two levels is **hysteresis**.

Sensor
A device which is used to monitor changes in the physical environment (*see also* transducer).

Sequence
A list of instructions in time order.

Signal
Information passing through an electronic system. Signals are usually changes in voltage.

Signal conditioning
Ensuring that the signal from one part of the system is within the acceptable range required by the next part of the system.

Sub-system
Part of a system which performs a particular function, an electronic building block.

Surface mounting
This is when the electronic components are soldered directly on to the copper tracks of the PCB. This is becoming standard practice in the electronics industry.

Syntax
The words, phrases and structure of the programming language.

System
All the following four points have to apply if something can be considered to be a system:

- the system is made up of parts or activities that do something,
- the parts or activities are connected together in an organised way,
- the parts or activities affect what is going through the system, so that it is changed when it leaves the system,
- the whole thing has been identified by humans as of interest.

(The Open University)

Transducer

Input – these respond to physical changes and produce electrical signals to represent these changes.

Output – these take electrical signals from the system and produce physical changes in the environment.

Voltage

The potential at a point in an electrical circuit – this is usually taken with respect to 0 volts or ground (earth).

Index